D1546899

HOW TO USE THE POWER OF PRAYER

by
Harold Sherman

Unity Books
Unity Village, MO 64065

How to Use the Power of Prayer was originally published by C & R Anthony, Inc., Publishers. First published in 1958. Six printings through 1974.

Second Printing 1986 by
Unity School of Christianity,
Unity Village, MO 64065

LLC: 85-051-703
ISBN: 87159-061-1

Introduction

The purpose of this book is to convince you that there is always an answer to prayer—when you have learned how to pray.

To get the right answer to prayer, you must know how to prepare your mind and heart so that you can enter consciously into the God-presence which exists within. Once this is accomplished—once you have felt this indescribable union with God, the Great Intelligence—if only for a fleeting, transcendent second—you will never be the same again.

You will know that God exists for you—the God of your faith, the God for whom you have searched, the one and only Power in this great and wonderful universe!

Harold Sherman

Table of Contents

I

Love—the Essential Key to Prayers

You are a product of love. You were conceived in love by your earthly father and mother. You were loved before you were born into this world. Loving preparations were made to care for you before your arrival. The first words ever spoken to you were, no doubt, words of endearment. You felt the warmth of your mother's breast, the deep peace and comfort and protection of her arms. And, as you grew in childish comprehension, you felt an increasing sense of security in the knowledge that your parents cared for you, that you could go to them when in trouble and that somehow they would make everything all right.

Not too many years after this, you began to realize that the love and understanding of your father and mother, however much it may have meant to you, was not enough. You discovered that even their love for each other was not quite sufficient for them. You found that they were reaching out as you had reached out when a babe—helpless and alone, save for them—seeking to find a higher love upon which they, too, could lean—the love of God.

Perhaps, if they came from religious backgrounds, they satisfied their inner longing by church affiliation. If so, your first concepts of God were formed through this association. You learned then that the simplest and yet the finest interpretation of the Creator of the universe could be expressed in three words: God is love.

When you thought of God as your heavenly Father, and you were told that you were made in His image, you could understand His love for you because you had known the love of an earthly father. Somehow, being able to picture God as a father made Him real and close and personal to you. You probably offered up your childish prayers with unquestioning faith. You loved God because He was supposed to protect you and give you the things you wanted. You may have feared

Him a little when you were naughty, but you knew God would forgive you if you asked Him, just as your own father would.

This relationship between God and yourself may have continued for some years. It may still exist. But the chances are, as you have matured through experience, your concept of God has changed. You may no longer think of God as an anthropomorphic being. You may regard Him now as infinite Spirit, Great Intelligence, Creator of an unthinkably vast cosmos, comprehensible only through His eternal laws and principles.

The magnitude of your present God-concept may have destroyed your childish faith. If you still pray, it may be more as a tribute, a recognition by you that some mighty, intelligent, creative force is behind all life and you must at least acknowledge it, even though you no longer believe in the existence of a personal God. To pray for help in meeting any of earth's problems may now seem futile, except as you know that any attempt to attain a peaceful, self-assured state of mind is always productive of good.

What your concept and whatever your attitude toward God at present, I want to give you the positive assurance that you can reestablish a personal feeling for God in a much more intimate, understanding, and demonstrable way than ever before. You can find God as I and millions of others have found Him—within your own mind and heart. You can become aware of God's presence when you have learned how to free your consciousness from fears and doubts and other disturbed thoughts, so that you can make contact with your real inner self and realize the miraculous fact that you actually are a part of God!

Science has revealed that, despite the different elements, there is only one basic substance in the universe and one Intelligence behind this substance, expressing itself through infinite forms and dimensions. The Bible tells us: " '*In him we live and move and have our being*'. . . . " (Acts 17:28) In this, science and religion are in agreement.

The great spiritual leaders throughout all time have sought to solve the mystery of God and creation. They have offered varying interpretations but have generally concurred that love, in its fullest and most unlimited meaning, is the greatest force in the universe, and that through love and love alone it is possible for us to express our feeling for God and sense His feeling for us in return. These spiritual leaders have emphasized, again and again, the individual as well as humankind's need of love—its power to heal, to protect, to inspire, to attract all manner of good things.

As you know, Jesus was asked: "*Teacher, which is the great commandment in the law?*" He replied: "*You shall love the Lord your God with all your heart, and with all your soul, and with all your mind*" and added that "*a second is like it, you shall love your neighbor as yourself.*" (Matt. 22:37, 39)

Jesus knew that if we observed these commandments the other commandments would take care of themselves. He knew that humans, with their heritage of animal instincts, were beset with fears, hates, suspicions, superstitions, resentments, jealousies, and other destructive passions which had made it difficult for them to develop and maintain love in their hearts and souls and minds for certain of their fellow humans or for God.

What was true in the time of Jesus is still true. You are a witness to "man's inhumanity to man," and you contribute to this inhumanity to the extent that you permit feelings of hate and prejudice and resentment and jealousy and suspicion of others and general negativity to exist in *your* consciousness.

Hate is the great destroyer—love is the great creator. You, as a creature of free will and free choice, may, any time you choose, exercise the power of hate or the power of love in your life.

If, under the influence of hate or other destructive feelings, you elect to misuse your God-given creative powers, God doesn't step in and warn you or try to drive out these wrong emotions. God knows that the only way you really learn the value of love is to have the experience of hate. You harm yourself every time you do not think and act in accordance with the physical, mental, and spiritual laws of the universe. Whenever things do not turn out right, it is not God's doing, it is your own. Somewhere along the line, you have failed to live in harmony with His laws—and the results are automatic, because you are living in a universe ruled by cause and effect.

Wrong thoughts infallibly produce wrong results just as right thoughts infallibly produce right results. In the realm of mind, like always attracts like. If you hate someone, you will attract hate in return. You cannot attract love with hate.

The spirit of evil is not an attribute of God. It is a creation of your own mind when you, as a creature of free will, elect to disobey God's laws. These laws are absolutely impersonal in their functioning. God plays no favorites with any member of creation, high or low, on any plane. Each form of life must earn its right to live and survive and evolve by its own efforts. God supplies all that is necessary for this living and surviving and evolving if His creatures only exercise the will and the intelligence to make the most of their God-given opportunities.

Jesus tried to make the people of His day understand that the kingdom of God is within, but few could really comprehend His great message. In the Lord's Prayer, He said again, "*On earth as it is in heaven.*" (Matt. 6:10) But, because most humans lacked inner vision, they looked for a heaven *outside* themselves, not realizing that heaven is actually a state of being.

When you are in harmony with the God consciousness within you—you are in heaven. When your mind and heart and soul are filled with love for others and for God—you are in heaven. When Jesus said: "*My kingship is not of this world,*" (John 18:36) He was referring to that eternal kingdom of oneness with God which exists within.

It is an incorruptible, indestructible kingdom. It has always existed and can never perish since you are a part of the God consciousness which created it. It was conceived in love and is eternally sustained by love. But you cannot enter this kingdom and experience its transcendent joys and indescribable bounties without love. Hate always drives you out of the kingdom, but love is the one unfailing key to your return.

Love is your only means of communication with God. Love is the highest, finest, most sublime feeling in the universe. Your capacity for love is unlimited, dependent upon the degree to which you can control your opposing feelings of hate, jealousy, resentment, prejudice, and all other destructive emotions to which you, as a human creature, are heir.

Why, you may ask, have you been born into a world of such sorrows and trials and hardships and disappointments and disillusionments and heartbreaks? Why, if God is love, has He permitted such evil things on this planet? Why the unbroken history of wars, the crimes of passion and violence, the unspeakable catastrophies of nature and of man? Why the bitter difficulties between even friends and loved ones? Why the wanton poverty, the savage competition, the monstrous economic inequalities between individuals and peoples? Why the crippling accidents of birth and life, the ravages of disease, the impairment of minds as well as bodies? Why, after all this must be endured, should it end in death? How can an all-merciful, all-loving God, Father of all, stand by and see His children lost in the wilderness of confused thoughts and feelings, seemingly unable to extricate themselves, without coming to their aid and setting things right?

"It is unthinkable," many have philosophized, "if a personal God possessing infinite compassion and love exists, that He would not have intervened on behalf of His long-suffering children."

On the surface, it would certainly appear that the Creator of this vast universe is not a God of love but a fiend incarnate! We, as earthly parents, would spare our children all that we possibly can of grief, unhappiness, and pain. This is our first instinct. Yet, the wisdom of our own experience teaches us that a too-protective attitude weakens rather than strengthens a child. If we do for the child what the child should do for himself, we rob that child of his individual development, his right to find himself and prove himself through his own self-assertion and self-expression.

We realize that we can best serve those we love by setting an example of right thought and right conduct, and giving them the free opportunity to pattern their lives after us in their own way. We know that if we encourage them to lean upon us, they are apt to be comparatively helpless when we are no longer with them. Would God exercise any less wisdom in giving us, His children, the freedom to develop our own powers of self-reliance and our individual ability to cope with the world within and without ourselves?

It has been said that "the worst affliction of all is never to have been afflicted." Can you appreciate the absence of pain, never having experienced pain? Can you know joy, never having undergone sorrow? Can you exult over a victory, never having tasted defeat? Can you rejoice in fulfillment, never having encountered disappointment? Can you value health, never having been ill? Can you judge what is good, never having encountered evil?

Look back over your life and you will see

that it has been filled with what might be called sins of omission and commission, mistakes you have made in thought and deed which have hurt others, as well as yourself. But, if you have reacted as you should toward these mistakes which produced unhappy results, you have grown by them. You are stronger in character because of them. You know now that you can face similar situations and deal with them in a constructive manner.

It has been said that life is a school containing many lessons. Many of these lessons are not learned easily or painlessly. So often, we are tempted to blame others and circumstances seemingly beyond our control for the things which have happened to us. We have filled our minds and hearts, as a consequence, with the destructive feelings of fear and hate and resentment. We have assumed bitter, unforgiving attitudes. We have prayed, if we have prayed at all, not that our shortcomings should be removed, but that our enemies should be destroyed. We have sought answers to our problems, not from within, but from without.

In such seeking, we have sought to express *our* will, and not God's, in our lives. We have made wrong use of His creative power by so doing, and have caused it to attract to us what we have not wanted. Each time you are impelled to action by hate, you can be certain that you are not acting in accordance with God's will and that the result cannot be good. If there dwells within your mind, at present, a deep hatred for some person or thing, you must remove it so that this hate can no longer stand between you and the right functioning of this God-power.

Love is the key to everything good and lasting in life. When it replaces your feelings of hate and other destructive emotions, you instantly feel a release of mind and body tensions. The conflicts within your consciousness cease, and you sense a union with a power greater than yourself, a power now freed to serve you constructively, to bring you the right answer to prayer as opposed to the wrong answers you have been getting when your consciousness has been dominated by wrong feelings.

To maintain love in your mind and heart, not only for your fellow creatures, but for God, is a difficult daily assignment, surrounded as you are by many who are living for themselves alone, who are out to get what they can any way they can, who will take advantange of you at every turn, who have few moral scruples and even less principle, and who are almost constantly—through their self-seeking, negative thinking—making wrong use of this God-given creative power. They have one objective in life—to *get.* Such people, it is true, often do get results on a material plane, not counting the cost in health or happiness or love and respect of others, or peace of mind. Only when life has punished them sufficiently does realization come that their way of thinking has not brought them the one thing they have really been trying to achieve—the inner security of knowing the love of someone near and dear to them, of having the capacity to love that person in return, and of experiencing the love of God.

Basically, whether or not any individual of any race or color or creed recognizes this deep inner urge, it is the quest of every human soul. Misguidedly, they may pursue a love of money, of things, of power, of position and prominence, of achievement—a love of anything and everything but the one, all-embracing love which, when it is possessed, causes all else in life to assume its rightful value and proportion. We may seek these other loves as a substitute but, once attained, we find that the inner satisfaction we thought would be experienced is still wanting.

True love must be shared; it cannot be hoarded. To be blessed by love, it must be expressed, not repressed. That is why the product of love is always good, and the product of hate is always evil. That is why God, the Great Intelligence, has permitted you, as a creature of free will and free choice, to discover this great truth for yourself—to learn the age-old lesson, forever new, that "as you sow, so shall you reap," either with love or with hate. You are never compelled to do right, but the power is always there for you to use rightly or wrongly, depending on your choice.

Perhaps now you can understand why it is imperative that your mind and heart be filled with love when you pray. It is not the words you use but the thoughts you think which influence the creative power within. People throughout all time have prayed for peace and cessation of war, but their prayers have not been answered. This is because the minds and hearts of most of them have been filled with hates and prejudices so that their prayers, however well-intentioned, were actually little more than lip service. Once having bestowed upon mankind the priceless gift of free will, God is helpless to assist until and unless we attune ourselves voluntarily to God's will, in obedience to His law.

So start now in preparation for the good things which will be set before your soul when you have illumined the path of your life by the light of love!

II

How Prayers Have Been Answered in Crises

It is instinctive for us, when we encounter conditions and circumstances beyond our control, to pray to a higher power for help. Believer and nonbeliever alike, when all earthly hope seems lost or when faced with a desperate situation, resort to prayer.

Deep in the mind and heart of every human creature there is the recognition of a Creator, a power in and above, to which we can turn when the burdens and pressures of this world become too much to face or endure on our own. There has not been a second of any day in any time since man became a self-conscious being, aware of the God-ward urge within, that countless millions of the species have not turned to God in prayer. This very minute, as you read these lines, millions of your fellow creatures throughout the world are praying.

Through this act of prayer they are recognizing that they, in themselves, are limited. They are seeking a wider horizon, a clearer perspective, a broader canvas upon which to view the problems of their lives. They are trying to free themselves from bondage of destructive thoughts and feelings so that they may know, without fear or prejudice, how to cope with whatever situation is confronting them. They are endeavoring to become conscious of what many describe as God's plan for them, by putting aside self that they may be guided in the right direction, thus avoiding, as far as possible, many of life's mistakes.

The urge to pray is always an urge for human betterment. It is the desire of the soul to be relieved of an unhappy situation or to be granted more of what that individual considers to be the good things of life. Many prayers, of course, are selfish or unwise, but no less fervent. The one who prays puts into his prayer the degree of feeling commensurate with the urgency of his need. "The facing of a great peril makes believers of us all," a veteran of Saipan and Inchon once said, in describing the occasions in which he and his buddies had faced possible death. "I know of no man, regardless of his faith or lack of faith, who did not pray in those times."

Historically, we have been told that George Washington prayed at Valley Forge, that Abraham Lincoln prayed in the darkest moments of the Civil War, that Woodrow Wilson and Franklin D. Roosevelt prayed in times of crisis. In fact, as exemplified by our leaders from the time of the birth of this country, there has been an increasing recognition that God must be given opportunity for participation in human affairs. It matters not what concept you or anyone else may have of God. If you appeal to this God-power within you, in the proper spirit, with sufficient faith and the willingness to follow direction from this higher source when the way is made clear to you, a right answer to prayer usually comes.

We often hear stories of dramatic answers to prayer. These are usually the most outstanding instances of such answers, and countless more, occurring daily, are never brought to public attention. But the evidence is overwhelming that something always happens when people pray, that a power within is activated, and that external circumstances and conditions begin to change even the relationships and attitudes between individuals.

An answer to prayer comes, irrespective of the religious faith or the age or intelligence of the person involved. A child's simple prayer can bring an answer as promptly and as definitely as an adult's. There is then, quite obviously, a universal creative source, or God-center, for want of any adequate words to describe this phenomenon, which responds infallibly and impersonally to the sincere petition of a human soul in need.

Here are a few examples illustrative of the way in which desperate needs have been answered through prayer.

One late afternoon, in West Roxbury, Massachusetts, J.S., forty-one, was welding a water pipe in the bottom of a ten-foot trench. There was a sudden cave-in of earth and rocks. He was jammed against the pipe in an upright position, his nose and an ankle broken. Somehow, as he had made a last frantic grab upward, his right arm had been caught in the slide, and his hand extended above the earth. His welding mask saved him from immediate suffocation. Unable to move, he tried to shout for help, but his voice could not be heard above the earth. With breathing difficult, J.S. decided to save his breath—and to pray.

The minutes dragged on as he kept repeating: "God, send someone please! God, send someone!" His broken nose was bleeding, and the blood was clotting in his throat, threatening to choke him.

Miles across town, his friend T.W. was driving home after work. A strange feeling suddenly gripped him. He felt a strong urgency to change direction, with his home only blocks away, and drive *six* miles at the height of the rush hour to have a look at the job where he knew J.S. had been working.

It had grown dark. Still impelled by this unexplainable feeling, T.W. arrived at the scene, jumped out of his truck, and noticed that the welder above the trench was still running. He thought someone must be down in the trench, working late, trying to finish the job. Nothing appeared to be unusual, but he crossed over and looked down into the trench, where he saw a man's hand projecting from the earth. He leaped down and began to dig and claw at the dirt. It was too solidly packed. Galvanized into action, he crawled from the trench, raced across the street to a garage, and came back with men and shovels.

Beneath this mound of earth, his friend, clinging desperately to consciousness, heard the sound of voices and felt the earth loosen around him. "Thank You, God," he said, and fainted.

The rescue squad arrived from the fire department with an oxygen mask, and he was revived. T.W. had saved the life of his friend because his mind had picked up the mental call for aid which J.S. had broadcast as he prayed.

A world champion pole-vaulter, B.R. declares that he has done things through prayer that otherwise would have been impossible. He credits prayer with having enabled him to make two of the greatest jumps of his life. One of these occasions was at a big meet in Finland, when he was stricken with strep throat two days before the event. The doctors shot him full of penicillin. He had little to eat, and was so weak the morning of the meet that it was difficult for him to do so much as a push-up. Despite this, the authorities requested him to put in an appearance at the track and make at least a token effort to compete.

B.R. prayed for strength, prayed not for

victory but that he might make the best showing possible. The competition began, and he cleared the bar his first few jumps, amazed that he had found the strength to do it. Finally, the bar was placed at just under fifteen feet—a height he had never jumped before. He stood for a moment at the starting line, holding his pole and eyeing the crossbar. Then he bowed his head and prayed for the strength to make one last jump. A sudden feeling of inexplicable power seemed to surge through his tired muscles. He lifted his pole and tore down the runway, vaulting up and over. As he fell into the sand pit, having cleared the greatest height of his career up to that time, he humbly and gratefully gave credit to God.

At another time, B.R. felt himself to be in no mental or physical condition to participate in the Chicago relays. He had to fly to the meet from Los Angeles and arrived at seven o'clock the night of the meet, with just time to get from the airport to the stadium to enter his event. But he had spent the time on the flight in prayer. It had seemed to him, tired as he was, that prayer would do him more good than sleep. He had learned through past performance that once his mind and body had been sufficiently conditioned by prayer, this higher power within supplied him with almost superhuman energy. That night, B.R. soared over the bar at a height of fifteen feet, four and seven-eights inches—just missing the world's record!

It is his conviction that when one believes in the power of prayer, one can accomplish what would ordinarily be considered as miracles.

The world is well acquainted with the inspiring saga of Captain Eddie Rickenbacker, who has relied again and again upon the power of prayer to see him safely through many crises in his life. When he was badly injured in a crash in one of his Eastern Airline planes some years ago, he heard a radio report from his hospital bed in Florida that he was dying. A tremendous urge to live welled up within him. He uttered a fervent prayer, "God, don't let me die!" and began to fight with all the force of body and will that he could command. Death released its grip upon him, and the indomitable Rickenbacker was back in his office within a few months.

Later, on a military mission during the Second World War, when his plane was forced down in the South Pacific, Eddie

Rickenbacker, through seventeen torturous days and nights, never lost faith that he and his companions would be rescued. Once, when they were out of food, a sea gull landed on his head and was captured. At other times, when the men were nearly frantic for want of water, sudden rain squalls developed, seemingly out of nowhere, and gave them sustenance. Finally, a Navy pilot, about to abandon his search, decided to turn back and circle one more area. It was then that he sighted Rickenbacker and his fellow survivors.

Rickenbacker declares that from the time he learned to pray at his mother's knee he has continued to pray about his personal and business problems, his friends, his family, and his country. He attributes his success in life, as well as his many miraculous escapes from death, to prayer.

Mrs. L.S., several years before her marriage, moved to California. One night a car in which she was riding with five other young people was hit by a Pacific electric train. Badly injured, she was taken to the hospital and x-rayed. The doctors told her, after a study of the X rays, that she would always have one leg shorter than the other and could never bear a child. They decided to place her in a cast the following day.

Left alone, a great and overwhelming prayer flooded her being: "Oh, God, help me, I must walk and I must be able to have a child!"

She held to this thought fervently, repeating the prayer over and over. The next morning, she determined to do something for herself before the doctors arrived. Making a supreme effort, she raised herself into a sitting position and then slowly slid her legs off the bed and stood on her feet. Her mother, watching from the doorway, saw her daughter do this, too astounded to move or cry out. From that moment on, Mrs. S. grew steadily better. A cast was never needed, and she fully recovered. She later married and had a healthy, normal child.

R.G., a driver for a Houston, Texas, trucking company, ran off the highway in his truck and crashed into a great oak tree in order to avoid a head-on collision with a drunken motorist. He was trapped in the cab. The steering wheel had smashed against his waist, and his feet were caught between twisted brake and clutch pedals. The doors of the cab were badly crushed and jammed—even a wrecking crew couldn't reach him. A fire was starting, there was no extinguisher, and the locked truck would soon be a mass of flames.

Helpless, as motorists, police, and others tried frantically to aid him, R.G. realized that he could survive only a minute or two at the most. In that moment, a giant man stepped forward and strode to the burning cab. He took hold of the door with both hands and wrenched it off, tearing it loose from the battered metal. Then he reached inside, ripped out the burning floor mat, and beat out the flames around R.G.'s feet with his bare hands. Next, grabbing the steering wheel, he bent it back from the victim's chest as though it were made of rubber. With cold precision, he took hold of the tangled brake pedal with one hand and the clutch with the other, and bent them back to free R.G.'s feet. But still it was impossible to get him out. The cab was smashed in and about him, top and bottom.

For a moment, the man stood back and surveyed the wreckage. To aghast onlookers, R.G.'s position looked hopeless. But the big man, with the sudden frenzied strength of ten men, leaped forward and literally drove his huge body into the cab beside the trapped driver, until he could press both feet solidly against the floor board. Hunched over in this position, he began to push and heave, the muscles of his back and arms straining under his torn shirt. Slowly, unbelieving onlookers saw the roof of the cab begin to lift. They heard the metal give under the terrific pressure the man was putting on it. Then, as he held the wreckage away from R.G., ready hands lifted the injured driver from the twisted debris. As soon as this was done, the man relaxed his herculean effort and lurched out of the cab just as what remained of the truck went up in flames.

In the excitement that followed, the heroic rescuer disappeared into the night his identity unknown. Later, he was found to be C.D.J., thirty-three, who had lost his first-born child in a fire which had destroyed his three-room house a little over a year before. He had saved four other children but had failed in his attempt to rescue his eight-year-old daughter when the house had exploded and knocked him unconscious.

Asked how he had been able to perform the prodigious feat of strength in his rescue of R.G. from the battered, fire-menaced cab of his truck, C.D.J. said simply, "I just prayed,

'God, help me get that man out of there!' "

H.E., nineteen-year-old son of Mrs. W.E., was returning home one night to their farm near Kirklin, Indiana, when he took a turn too fast and skidded off the road. His car overturned in a dry creek bed, out of sight from the highway. He was pinned beneath it.

At four o'clock in the morning, when her son failed to return home, Mrs. E. began touring the country roads in search of him. She felt, somehow, that he had been in an accident and was calling her. After covering many miles, she came to a bridge with fresh skid marks at the approach. Getting out of her car, she followed the dry creek bed until she came to her son's overturned automobile. He had been under his wrecked car for seven hours when she found him, and his first words were, "I knew you'd come, Mom. I've been praying for you to find me—but it sure took you a long time."

C.L.R., forty-three, of Hot Springs, Arkansas, was prospecting for uranium with another man along the Colorado River. They became lost and separated, each going in a different direction. For eight days he wandered about, living on small lizards. With tin cans, he tried to signal planes that flew over. When motorboats went by, he threw rocks and yelled, but their occupants never saw him, even though he jumped in the river and tried to swim toward them. He had a Bible with him, and kept praying that someone would see him or find him. On a day when it seemed that he couldn't survive another night, having lost forty-two pounds and reached a state of almost complete exhaustion, he opened the Bible at random to a passage which read, as he interpreted it, "And the good Lord will not give you any more than you can endure." Shortly thereafter, following another period of prayer, C.R. heard a boat which contained a searching party, and he was sighted. He blacked out as he was picked up but, on returning to consciousness, said that he was sure his prayers for rescue had been answered because he hadn't ever lost faith, even when his condition had seemed all but hopeless.

Observe that all these people in trouble knew what they had to have to save them.

J.S., buried in the trench, prayed, "God, send me someone!"

B.R., before his pole-vault competition, prayed: "God, give me strength!"

Eddie Rickenbacker, broken in body as a result of a plane crash, prayed, "God, don't let me die!" Later, when down in the South Pacific ocean, he prayed, "God, care for us. Give us food and water and let us be found!"

In each case, the person praying was specific in his or her petition. Each of them, and every person whose prayer has been answered, has prayed for something *definite.* They have known what they have wanted and needed to meet a certain situation, however critical, and they have pictured this need in their mind's eye with great intensity while praying.

Once this was done, the God-power within took over, attracting to them the help needed, and giving them the physical and mental strength to help themselves as far as possible. These dramatic answers to prayer, after they have taken place, always appear miraculous—as, indeed, they are. Let's analyze the case histories which have been described in this chapter so that we can fully understand and appreciate the miracles produced by prayer.

When J.S. was buried by the slide of dirt in the trench, his life depended upon someone coming to the scene and discovering his plight. While there were people in the vicinity, they were busy with their own affairs. There was nothing in sight to indicate to them, had they looked, that anything was wrong. When he commenced praying for help, imploring God to send someone, the God-power within knew that the mind of a friend who had a *feeling* for him had to be reached.

The skeptic might say, "If there is a God mindful of our difficulties, who can and does act in our behalf in answer to prayer, why didn't He exercise His power and lift the earth off J.S.?" But the God of this universe is a God of law and order who works through us and not through personal intervention. No law is ever set aside to meet a human need. But laws with which we are yet not too familiar are often set in motion as we make urgent calls upon the God-power within.

In families where emotional ties are strong, many sense when another loved one is in trouble. H.E.'s mother was the logical one to respond to his need, when and if her mind could be reached and impressed. He was concentrating upon her to the exclusion of everyone else. In the case of J.S., he prayed to God to send "someone," not specifying who that someone might be. It was then up to the God-power within to find *the* someone who would respond, and his friend proved to be the one. Had H.E. *not* fixed his mind exclusively on his mother, it is possible that God-power within him would have impulsed some other person or passerby to notice the skid marks on the road and to investigate.

If your directions to this God-power are too specific, you sometimes limit its functioning for you because it has to work through you and through the minds of others to provide the answer you need. Sometimes it is better to express your need and to let this God-power determine the ways and means and the sources of supply, because it can reach out and make contacts which are entirely beyond your conscious knowledge or your awareness.

C.L.R., prospector, carried his Bible with him on his expeditions. He had need of it on the occasion when he became lost in the wilds along the Colorado. Planes passed over and motorboats occasionally roared by on the river, without their occupants seeing him. After eight days, he was almost starved and near complete exhaustion. His prayer had been that he would stay alive until found. He read his Bible and was sustained by the thought that "God would not tempt him beyond his endurance." C.L.R.'s faith in the Bible added faith to his prayers. He was willing to help himself as much as he could by catching and eating small lizards. Had he not been willing to make this effort, God might not have answered his prayer to keep him alive. The answer came in the form of a suggestion that he feed on these lizards. It was a distasteful thought, which he had to overcome. Had he rejected this idea, it is possible he might not have had the strength to survive.

When you have prayed for help in a desperate situation and unusual ideas come to you, you must be prepared to act upon them. Many people have received answers to prayer in this manner, but because the answers have seemed so extraordinary and unconventional, they have never recognized them.

Again, it is necessary to emphasize that God works through existing forms of life and things on this earth in the answering of prayer, whether it be a lizard, or a sea gull, or a rain squall, or the right man or woman in the right place at the right time, or the inner urge to do the right thing yourself. It is all a manifestation of the unlimited variety of ways that God employs in the answering of prayer. Since anything and everything is a part of God, He can manifest through any form that is most expedient at the moment.

You should, therefore, take new courage and faith from the realization that, if God can serve you as dependably and as effectively in times of great crisis, how much more may you rely upon His care and guidance if you seek it in your everyday problems.

III

How to Prepare Your Mind for Prayer

A wise gardener prepares the soil before he plants the seed. One who prays must prepare his mind to receive that which he plants in the form of a prayer. He must weed out from the soil of his mind the wrong chemical elements of fear and doubt and other disturbing emotions, then energize his mental soil with desire and fertilize it with faith, in order to provide the conditions upon which the God-power within can act and help bring what is prayed for into material manifestation.

God cannot help you unless you make clear to Him what help you want. Since you have been created a creature of free will and free choice, it is up to you to decide and then to ask, in accordance with God's law: "*Ask and it will be given you. . . .*" (Matt. 7:7) But you must first *ask*—and you must know not only how to ask, but what to ask for, in order to receive the right answer to prayer.

If you have more than one need or desire in your mind at a time, and if these needs or desires are in conflict, you cannot present a strong and vivid picture of what you want. The God-power within is ready and willing to serve you at all times, but when your prayers are clouded by confusion and indecision, and the mental pictures of what you want are weakened by fears that you won't get it, you cannot expect to make sufficient union with the God-power to get a satisfactory or even intelligent answer to prayer.

Each time you pray you will get some kind of an answer, because the God-given creative power within will respond to your expressed desires, however ineffective and misguided and unreasonable or foolish these desires may be.

You will always get in your outer life what you have put into your inner life, because things happen in the mind before they can happen in the world without.

A gardener plants a seed in the darkness beneath the surface of the earth. You plant a desire in the dark room of your inner mind, where it takes root and grows, developed by the creative power acting upon the mental picture you have planted. Eventually, what you have pictured begins to manifest itself, bit by bit, in your outer life, until it becomes fully materialized, exactly as you have pictured it from the beginning. If your visualization has been faulty or incomplete, what is manifested will contain the same imperfections and incompleteness.

You, within certain limitations, are the creator of your own destiny. The old saying that "God helps those who help themselves" is eternally true. God does not step in and correct your confused thinking or check your wrong desires. This is your end of the joy. He lets you learn by experience what is right and what is wrong, what is good or bad for you.

Gradually, as you are punished by your wrong desires and mistakes, you discover what is best for you, what you really want in life, and how to ask for it in prayer.

In other words, you improve your relationship with this God-power within, you find how to attune yourself to it. You do this by first eliminating all disturbed thoughts, by putting aside all selfish desires, by asking for the kind of help that can bring only good, only the highest, to you and to others.

There is no real happiness to be attained in taking advantage of another, in getting away with something you know is not right, in achieving a goal you have not earned. It may have seemed easier to obtain what you wanted in this manner, and yet you have evidence that each time you have been tempted to do so, you have laid yourself open to others treating you as you have treated them.

Wrong operation of your God-given creative powers cuts you off from all protection by the God-power within. When you elect to misuse this power, it cannot keep you from suffering the consequences of your own destructive thoughts and desires, for if God controlled your every thought and act, and kept you from having a wrong thought or making a wrong move, you would never develop any strength of character or ability in and of yourself. You would be like a puppet on a string, and yours would be a senseless, useless existence.

You could have no respect for yourself, and God, your Creator, would take no delight in a creature dependent solely upon Him. There would be no purpose in creating a creature incapable of functioning by itself. But God, like an earthly father, does not abandon His creation. He has, instead, placed a part of Himself in each of His creatures so that He can be in position to guide and to help when they learn of His presence in their consciousness and how to call upon it through uniting their thoughts with Him in prayer.

This is one of the great miracles in life. Jesus tried to convey to us our coexistence with God when He said: "... *I am in the Father and the Father in me.*" (John 14:10) He repeatedly stated that we were all "*sons of God,*" indicating a genuine kinship which can only exist in consciousness.

God never disowns us, but we often disown God by wrong thinking and desires. You can tell when you are out of attunement with the God-power by the way you inwardly feel. You may deceive others, but you cannot deceive yourself, and you can never fool the God-power within.

This Power knows whether or not you mean what you pray. You may have a fine choice of words, your prayer may be delivered with what sounds like great fervor and sincerity, but it is the real inner feeling that counts. If in your innermost heart and mind you lack conviction, if you are not honest with yourself or with God, if you are not truly presenting your problems, you will not be able to impress the God-power within to act in your behalf.

Some people have formed such a habit of right thinking that it has become second nature to them. They sense immediately when they "get off the beam," and get busy changing their mental attitude. But this life has so many testing experiences that it is difficult for even the most balanced man or woman to maintain mental and emotional control at all times. To the degree that this can be done, however, just to that degree will they remain in attunement with the God consciousness. Such attunement assures them far greater peace of mind, happiness, health, and all-around security than those who only occasionally make contact with this God-power.

Imagine yourself as a small local power station that has a connection with the big central power plant any time you wish to switch it on. Instead, you try to get along on just the power you've got within yourself. You haven't realized how much and how easily you could vastly increase this power if you would hook up to it through prayer. You have marveled at friends who somehow found the power to meet situations that you couldn't meet. You have thought, mistakenly, that they had something in them you didn't have. The only difference between you and these friends has been that they had learned to use this power of God within them, to turn it on when needed, while you have passed it up, have seldom if ever consciously, deliberately drawn on this great reserve to help you solve problems beyond the capacity of your own mind to solve.

How, then, do you prepare your mind for prayer? You do it, automatically, at times, when under the pressure of a great emergency. You forget the existence of your physical body; you make your conscious mind, with its ordinary fears and worries, passive; you turn the full attention of your entire being inward, concentrating only upon your need of the moment, picturing what that need is, and crying out, with the deepest possible feeling, "God, help me!" The urgency of the situation is so great that your call for help goes direct to that portion of God, the Great Intelligence which exists within you, and registers the need with it.

The instant God-power is reached, it goes

into action, as it has in the emergency cases related in the previous chapter. In ways which cannot be put into adequate words, ways which cannot be comprehended, conditions are magnetized around you. The God-power takes over and reaches out through time and space when necessary to impress other minds with your need, to attract help to you. If it is only the right move to make to avoid a serious accident on a highway, the impulse is given you in an intuitive flash. You make this move almost subconsciously, and wonder afterward why you did it, when any other move would have been the wrong one and might have meant possible death to yourself and others.

Here you have evidence of the instant working of the God-power within you. But you may have found, when you have everyday needs which are not so urgent, that you have difficulty reaching the God consciousness through prayer. Even your faith that God can and will help you is lacking. You are self-conscious about the whole subject of prayer. Your mind has time to mull things over, and it begins to talk back to you, saying, "Maybe the times you think you were helped were just coincidences. Maybe if you hadn't prayed for help, you'd have gotten out of those jams just the same. Maybe it was your own mind that did the job after all. Why should God be interested in your little problems?"

If you have been besieged with these skeptical, doubting thoughts and feelings, you know that they can keep you from praying with real faith and conviction. No prayer will be answered unless it has the power of genuine belief behind it. It is a waste of time to pray when you know you are only giving lip service to it.

Do you take a friend seriously when you know he doesn't mean what he is saying? Then why expect the great God-power within you to act in your behalf when you have little or no faith in what you are doing or in your ability to get an answer to prayer?

A.J.B. and his wife, of Eugene, Oregon, lived a life of prayer. Mr. B. as a young boy of eight living in Nova Scotia, started praying for help when he and his mother and sister were snowed in, and the father had gone to town and was unable to get back home to them with food. There were no snow plows in those early days. Their food and water were gradually exhausted. The cabin was entirely covered with snow, over six feet deep on the level.

Mr. B. told me that he remembers as though it were yesterday how he got down on his knees with his mother, and how they prayed to God to open up some way for them to get food and keep them until Father got home.

The storm, which had been raging unabated for a number of days, began to clear. The sun came out. Mr. B. ventured to open the door and saw the snow packed in a solid wall over the house. He shoveled some of it into an iron pot. His mother melted it over a fire in the fireplace, and they each had a drink. Then the eight-year-old dug some steps in the snow and cautiously climbed up on top to look over the fields. To his amazement, he saw a girl coming across the snow on snowshoes. She had a sack of something in her arms.

"I told Mother," he related, "and she said to me to stay on top of the snow till she came, and then try to get her down the snow steps I had made. We didn't have any snowshoes in the house, and no one could get anywhere without them.

"When the girl, fourteen-year-old T.P., got down into our house, she said that her mother had sent her over from their home, over a mile away, with ten pounds of corn meal, to trade with my mother for a skein of yarn, as she was weaving some cloth and ran short of yarn to finish it. They hadn't realized we were in such a desperate state, or that Father wasn't home. The trade was made. I helped the girl back up on the snow, and she started back to her house. I then went down the snow steps and joined Mother in the house, and we got down on our knees and thanked God for sending the meal. Mother made a nice thick corn cake, and we all had the cake and snow water for supper. That was the best corn cake I ever ate in my life, and Mother said it was because the meal came from God. We had no meat, vegetables, or milk; everything had been eaten up and we had begun to feel the pinch for food when the girl came—just because her mother suddenly felt she had to have that yarn, regardless of how snowbound everything was!

"Father didn't get back till some days later, bringing some corned beef, brown sugar, and oatmeal. He was almost exhausted even then, getting through the snow, as the roads were not cleared and he had sunk in up to his armpits in places. Naturally we all got down on our knees and thanked God again. That experience proved to me, as a boy, that God does answer prayer, and from that time on, I always went to God when I was in trouble."

Mr. B. related one experience after another, throughout his life, when he had been faced with a real need, after having done all he humanly could to solve his own problems. Then, when he had felt that a certain problem was beyond him, that he would have to ask God to give him a lift, he has gone off by himself to "talk it over with God and explain to Him what I had to have."

"Never," he testified, "has God failed me when I have been really up against it. I haven't bothered God with trifles. I figure God expects a person to do what he can to help himself. But I've never hesitated to go to God for aid when I know I've done my best and I still haven't gotten anywhere."

God, to Mr. B., was a very real power. He was confident that God was always present and that he could always be reached. His belief in God's power was unquestioning.

The need for financial help is common. We

have all encountered economic difficulties when we needed immediate cash to see us through a business or personal crisis. If we have prayed over it, doubting that any help would be forthcoming, we have usually only made matters worse.

"I knew God wouldn't answer my prayer. He never has," a businessman said to me once, when faced with possible bankruptcy.

I tried to make him see that his lack of faith had made it impossible for the God-power to do anything for him.

"What's faith got to do with it?" he demanded. "If God is an omnipotent, all-merciful God, He knows I'm in trouble and He should help me whether I have faith or not. Then maybe I *would* have faith in Him!"

This copartnership with God is not a one-way street. Faith is the price you have to pay to get right answers to prayers. It is the one element or force which closes the gap between your own real self and the God Presence within. Faith brings our power and the power of God together on the human level so that God can work through us and help us achieve what we wish or need.

Had this man exercised the faith of Mr. B., his prayer for financial relief would have been answered. The following example, again taken from Mr. B.'s experience, demonstrates the right approach to God when faced with financial need.

"It was in 1907," related Mr. B. "I had built a saw manufacturing plant, and had been running it for about six months, when my bookkeeper came to me on Friday noon, and said, 'There is a carload of grind stones at the depot, with seven hundred dollars freight due, which must be paid tomorrow, before noon. Not only that, we will have to pay the man three hundred dollars in wages. I have used up all our money, and we won't have any coming in for two weeks. You are the manager. It's up to you to dig up the cash to pay these pressing bills.'

"I left the shop and went home on the streetcar to dinner. I told my wife that I had to get a thousand dollars before noon tomorrow. She said to me, 'If you have the faith that you told me your mother had in God, I suggest that you go upstairs to your bedroom and pray to God to open up some way so you can get the thousand dollars on time.'

"I said to her, 'That's just what I'm going to do', and when I came downstairs, my wife asked, 'Do you think you'll get it?' I said,

'Yes, dear, I think I will.'

"I walked out of our house and went down to Granville Street for about two blocks, and a butcher came out of the Vancouver Hotel and said, 'Hello, Mr. B.! How are you getting along?'

"I said, 'The mill men are patronizing our business very well. In fact, I have more business right now than I have the capital to handle it.'

"He said, 'Come with me to my office. I have something I want to give you.' We both took the streetcar to his office and he told his bookkeeper to make me a check for a thousand dollars and that I would send back a thousand dollars' worth of my company's stock for it.

"I returned to my shop in a little less than an hour and handed my bookkeeper the check. He said, 'In the name of God, how did you get it?' I said, 'I got it in the name of God.' And he said, 'If I had that much faith in God, I would quit the saw business!' This is positively a true story. My good wife is a witness to it."

No one who has had similar experiences with the power of prayer will doubt Mr. B.'s story. I have had many of my prayers answered. But, like Mr. B., I have realized that I must put aside my fears and worries before I go to God in prayer. One must have a clear channel in consciousness through which the God-power can work.

Let's go back now and analyze what happened when Mr. B. prayed to God to enable him to get the money he needed. Mr. B. felt the urge to walk down Granville Street. The God-power synchronized his movements in time so that he just "happened" to run into the butcher, who just "happened" to ask him how he was doing, which gave Mr. B. the opportunity to say that he was doing fine, only he needed a little capital. And then the butcher, with no prompting from Mr. B., invited him to come to the office to pick up a check for a thousand dollars—the very sum he had told God he had to have! But, in ways we cannot understand, this butcher's mind had been reached and prepared to render this service. Call it telepathy; call it a communication between the part of God in one man and the part of God in the butcher. Explain it any way you will—the connection with these two men was made, first mentally, then physically, and the prayer was answered.

Mr. B. did not think of the butcher while he

was praying or at any other time. He told God of his need in prayer, and the God-power within brought him in touch with the one person who could help him.

When God answers prayer it is always done easily and naturally, without strain, however accidental or coincidental or even impossible it may seem on the surface.

I was in a similar predicament a few years ago in Hollywood. A writing assignment on which I had counted fell through and left me temporarily stranded. I needed the same sum—a thousand dollars. There was no one I knew on the Coast to whom I could go for aid. At that time writers, however much money they may have made, could not get a loan at a bank without cosigners, since they were not employed by a business house and had no salary or regular income to back them up.

I spent a night in prayer. I needed this thousand dollars at once. I did not try to think of any person to whom I could go. I just saw, in my mind's eye, myself being led to someone who would advance me this amount of money—with God's help.

The next morning I arose with a feeling of expectancy. I did not know from what source the money would come, but I felt that something had happened while I slept, and that all I had to do was to await developments, not permitting any fear or worry to demagnetize the conditions that had been established. This is where many people undo the power of prayer. An answer may be on the way, but they lose their faith, and this instantly begins to change the conditions that prayer has set up for them.

Faith in prayer must persist, not just while you are praying but until the answer comes. If you permit your fears and doubts to take over and say to you, "But your prayer hasn't been answered yet. How do you know it will be? Time is running out. You've got to do something. What are you going to do?" Then these fears and doubts will defeat you.

How well I know how hard it is to control your mind and your emotions, to maintain your faith, when you are under cruel pressure. This doesn't mean you shouldn't keep on trying in every way possible to help yourself. But, after you have prayed for help, you may be inspired to take some steps by the God-power which will lead you to the answer you seek.

Mr. B. had to walk down Granville Street

to find his answer waiting for him in the person of the butcher. I awakened in the morning after my prayer with the feeling that I must wait where I was, in my Hollywood apartment, for help.

Around ten-thirty in the morning, the phone rang. It was Wesley Barr, managing editor of the Los Angeles *Herald-Express,* a man I had only recently met when he had interviewed me concerning my experiments in long-distance telepathy with Sir Hubert Wilkins. During the course of the conversation, he asked, out of a clear sky, "Sherman, is there anything I can do for you?"

"Yes," I said, on impulse, as my inner voice instructed. "I need a thousand dollars. Can you help me get it?"

"I'll call you back in ten minutes," he said. In five minutes, Barr was back on the phone. "You are to have lunch in downtown Los Angeles at the Jonathan Club with Eugene Overton, a friend of mine," he said. "Tell him what you need and why you need it. It's all fixed."

I kept this appointment and met a most unusual man, one of the best-known and best-loved attorneys on the West Coast. He is my attorney as I write this, and he may be somewhat embarrassed when he knows I have put this experience in print. He handed me—a man he had never seen before—a check for one thousand dollars in answer to my need, simply on the word of Wesley Barr, who scarcely knew me himself!

Yes, God answers prayer—if you know how to prepare your mind to receive.

In your consciousness there is a point where your own thinking leaves off and the Intelligence that is God begins. Therefore, in order for you to knowingly receive guidance and protection from God, you must develop the ability to sense this point of contact, in consciousness, with Him.

How is this done? I discovered a way during my experiments with Sir Hubert Wilkins. These long-distance telepathy experiments, as you may know, were conducted under scientifically controlled conditions, at a time when we were separated by some three thousand miles. Sir Hubert was in the north polar regions and I, acting as receiver of his thoughts, was in the study of my New York City apartment. The experiments demonstrated, as has been proved many times before and since, that under certain conditions—requiring relaxation of body and mind—it is possible for man to communicate mind to mind.

But here is a tremendously reassuring and comforting fact that is not generally realized: there need be no separation between man and God in consciousness! You can communicate, through your mind, with the mind of God! This was my discovery: that the same technique I had used for reaching the mind of Wilkins was the most effective method for communicating mind to mind with the God-power within me!

To reach the mind of Wilkins and attune my mind to his, I had to create in my consciousness a strong desire for communication. I had to have the unquestioning faith that I could make this contact. This meant that my own mind had to be freed of all fears, apprehensions, and doubts. Once this was done and I had concentrated my full attention upon Wilkins, completely relaxed, physically and mentally, I could *feel* my mind, on a subconscious level, touch Wilkins' mind.

I wish it were possible to convey this feeling in words. Have you ever felt that someone was thinking strongly of you? It is an unmistakable feeling when it comes, and you are thrilled when you have it proved to you that a loved one or friend was actually thinking of you at the precise moment. You may not have been able to explain how it happened, but you have had demonstrated to you, in that instant, that thoughts and feelings can be transmitted and received.

When you desire to make contact with the God-power within, have faith that this feeling of closeness to God will come to you. At first, you may only sense it for a fleeting instant, as contact with this God Presence is made. But, with continued meditation, you will be able to "close the circuit" between your mind and God's mind, almost at will. Then is the time, when you have had this uplifted feeling, for you to give utterance to your prayer, and picture in your mind's eye what you desire to come to pass for which you need God's help.

When you are up against a difficulty which seems beyond your power to meet or solve, then is the time to get off by yourself and attempt to quiet your mind and your nerves. Realize that your fears and worries have no power to solve anything. As long as you give them control over you, you will be powerless to get an answer to prayer.

You must first make your mind receptive

by letting go of these fears and worries—by letting yourself be conscious of one great reassuring fact: you are not alone. A part of God, the Great Intelligence, dwells within you. You can call upon this God-power to guide and protect you any time you need, once you put aside the barriers of fear and worry.

The physical attitude you take in prayer is unimportant. If you have been accustomed to praying on your knees and feel natural in this position, then assume it. If you feel more comfortable praying while seated or while lying down, then follow this procedure. Whatever physical or mental positions you have found enable you to relax physically and mentally and to reach a state of deep meditation—that's the method you should use.

The suggestions given here are meant only as a supplementary aid for you to utilize if you need it.

To reach this God-power, sit by yourself in a chair, or stretch yourself out upon a sofa or bed. Repeat these words to yourself, and cause yourself to do and feel what the words suggest:

I let the chair (or sofa or bed) hold my

entire weight.

I now relax my body—all physical tenseness is gone.

I turn my attention inward—and become unself-conscious of my body.

I now feel that I exist only in consciousness.

A feeling of great inner quiet and peace begins to come over me.

In this moment of quiet—this inner stillness—I now give expression to my prayer, describing in words and also presenting in mental picture form, what I feelingly desire.

Then, through an exercise of faith, I set up in myself a confident expectation that what I have visualized will come to pass in my life—that all the resources and developments I need are on their way to me in time—as an answer to prayer.

Practice this technique until it becomes subconscious with you. In this way, you will eventually be able to relax body and mind and make yourself ready for prayer at a moment's notice, whenever the need arises.

In order to pray effectively, you must learn how to harness faith to prayer. When you are by yourself, preferably selecting a quiet time each day when you can sit and meditate, you should repeat the following words, giving deep thought to their meaning, until they become a part of your consciousness:

I fully understand that faith, expressed through prayer, is the deep, unassailable inner feeling that, through God's guidance and help and my own earnest effort, what is right for me will come to me.

I realize that, to attain an answer to prayer, I must have faith in myself and in God.

I know that faith is the activator of my God-given creative power and that, to exercise real faith, I must first eliminate all doubts and fears.

I further realize that, when I pray, I must hold and maintain the genuine conviction that what I desire can and will come to pass—has even now been created in mind—and only awaits the right time to materialize as an actual happening in my life.

I recognize that only to the degree that I can keep a clear mental picture of what I desire in mind, and support it by my faith, will this picture become a reality.

You can achieve seeming miracles when you have learned how to couple faith with prayer. But you must also thoroughly understand what prayer is and what prayer does for you.

Here, vitalized, so you can make this awareness a part of your consciousness, are affirmations designed to help you develop the power of prayer. Repeat these affirmations until they are indelibly impressed upon your subconscious:

I know that everything that comes to me in the world without first has to be created for me in the world within.

This creation takes place in prayer through the interaction of my mind with the God-given creative power which is always ready to serve me in accordance with the nature of my thoughts and desires.

Prayer, supported by faith, overcomes wrong mental and emotional conditions within me, and places me in harmony with the God-power.

Only through daily attunement with

God-consciousness and an expressed desire to live up to the best that is in me can I be assured of inner guidance and protection.

I therefore resolve to make prayer a vital part of my everyday life, realizing how essential it is to my well-being in every way.

When you have fully comprehended these affirmations and made them a part of your consciousness, you can begin to pray with the assurance that your prayers will be answered, and that you can make knowing contact with the God Presence within you at will.

IV

How to Pray for Others

You are assuming quite a responsibility when you pray for another. Perhaps you have always included members of your family in your prayers with the usual request that God will protect them and keep them. This has become what amounts to a ritual with you. Your prayer is very much the same each night. You pray more from a sense of habit and duty than from any feeling of urgency. It is only when a loved one is taken ill or is injured, or in some sort of trouble or danger, that your prayer concerning him takes on a deeply earnest quality. Then you wish to be sure to impress God with the need for His care and protection, so you put your whole heart and mind behind the prayer. Your assumption is that when everything is right with your loved ones, God's help is not especially required.

Actually, we each need at all times the guidance and protection which continued contact with the God-power within can give us, no matter how smoothly life appears to be running on the surface. Even in its happiest, seemingly most secure moments, life is uncertain. You can take a boat trip in safety without a life preserver, but in case of accident a life preserver is a handy thing to keep you afloat until help comes.

The right kind of prayer, for yourself or for anyone else, can prove a life preserver in many instances. It is better never to be without prayer and the true spirit of prayer. If you pray merely from custom, without putting genuine thought and feeling behind it, your prayer will have no impact upon the God consciousness. It might as well be so much mumbo-jumbo.

Make this a rule: never pray unless you mean it. And even though you may repeat essentially the same prayer or prayers over and over, put real feeling into them. It is more important to help keep your loved ones well and safe than it is to help get them restored to health after something has happened.

Prayer does and can help! The God-power within is reactive to the thoughts and feelings of others directed toward an individual. In some way that we cannot understand, but which has been demonstrated again and again, your mind is joined with the mind of the person for whom you are praying. This union takes place on subconscious levels. Neither the pray-er nor the object of his prayers is ordinarily consciously aware of this mental contact. It is possible that the communication is set up between the God-power in you and the God-power in the other person. Something leaves you which is received by the other. If your prayer has been selfless, inspired only by the desire to help a friend or loved one, it can accomplish great good. But if your prayer has been motivated by a desire to bring about a change which is pleasing or beneficial to you, and not necessarily the kind of change that would be best for the individual, you can cause great harm.

I have consulted with many men and women who have been hurt by the well-intentioned prayers of designing or overindulgent, overpossessive members of their families. It is easy for a mother or father to think they know what is best for their erring children. In such cases, many seek to dominate or dictate through prayer. This always leads to unhappy results, because sons and daughters rebel against attempts to direct their lives by invoking the aid of God to "make them see the light"—or do what a parent may want them to do.

"I hate prayer!" an alcoholic once said to me bitterly. "My mother has prayed for me all her life. She prayed that I would be a good boy . . . that I wouldn't get into trouble . . . that I'd stop smoking and swearing and drinking . . . that I wouldn't marry the girl I wanted to marry because she thought she wasn't the right one . . . that I'd get a job near home so I could stay with her . . . that I would come to see that her plans for me were right . . . and that I would stop trying to go against her advice. Oh, no, you don't get me mixed up in prayer. It's already ruined my life!"

This mother undoubtedly thought she was doing the best she knew how for her boy. She probably couldn't understand why God was not answering her prayers. She didn't realize that she was trying to impose her will upon her son—and that even God does not impose His will upon any human creature. It is up to each individual to make his will God's will, by an act of submission. There is no compulsion about it.

This son had deeply resented his mother's lifelong effort to run his life. The more she prayed for him, the more he resisted her impassioned thoughts and feelings, which reached his consciousness but were repelled. His revolt took the form of a rebellion not only against his mother, but against God. He looked upon prayer as a vicious tool by which his mother was seeking to work the power of God on him. As a result, this man was driven to excessive drinking and to destructive acts. He hated his mother, he hated God, he reached the point where he didn't care whether he lived or not.

The world is, unhappily, full of such examples—perhaps not as extreme, but just as misguided—wherein friends and loved ones have thought they were helping by telling God what *they* wanted to have done for another in prayer, instead of asking God to do what He felt was best. You may think you know the answer to another's problem, but you cannot know precisely how this person thinks or feels and whether or not your answer would be accepted by him as his answer.

Therefore it is a mistake to pray for this answer, unless you know that he is in agreement, and, if cooperative, is praying for the same answer himself.

You can be certain that your prayer will be helpful if you pray for the good of another person, if you do not inject yourself into the picture and try to play the role of God.

Your God-power and this individual's God-power possess an awareness of what needs to be done to provide the right answer to prayer, where you do not. Therefore, it is best to imagine the removal of whatever difficulty this friend or loved one is facing, without trying to determine the specific way in which this is to be done. This procedure is up to the individual himself, aided by that God-power which dwells in him and which may be activated to serve him partially as a result of your earnest, prayerful petitions. Any recipient of prayers in his behalf must make an effort to help himself. On many occasions, conditions improve enough as a result of these prayers, so that he gains the courage and faith to get back on his own feet. When you pray that a person will have the strength and the wisdom to do what is best for him and for others involved, you are helping him get a new hold on himself.

A sixty-three-year-old woman who worked for a real estate firm in a Midwestern state, wrote to tell me of her experiences in praying for others. She did not wish her name mentioned because she felt that this would limit her effectiveness if people learned that she was praying in their behalf. But this woman was in a position to know when payments on homes were due and when certain families were undergoing economic crises. She sympathized with their needs and helped in the only way possible to her—through prayer.

Finding that the maid serving the real estate company shared her faith in prayer, the two women decided to combine their forces. Here, in this woman's own words, is the account of how they operated.

"The maid and I have long, long talks on matters deep to our hearts, and we have joined in prayer more than once to help some unfortunate family that didn't know where the next payment on their home was coming from. The wonders we have witnessed in the rehabilitation of these people—most of them unknown to us if we could meet them on the street, or just voices to me on the telephone—would be difficult for the average person to believe. I do what I can, where I can, and a very humble vessel am I to carry on my Lord's work. But no one can shake my faith in prayers rightly held and given out. I have seen too many miraculous answers, always coming from a direction least expected."

Notice this last significant statement: ". . . always coming from a direction least expected." This is usually the way it happens when you have prayed as you should, not trying to force anyone you know, in your prayer, to do what you want or to help you—but leaving it up to the God-power within to work through whatever person or persons He selects.

These two women were fulfilling the law of prayer by praying, not for themselves, not for any personal gain or motive, but completely, selflessly, for others. And these people were receiving the full impact of their unselfish petitions, their own God-power influenced to act for their good by the God-power in the consciousness of those who were praying for them!

There are times when others have more faith in you and your prayers than they have in themselves and their own prayers. In these cases, they make their minds receptive to help and put aside their own fears and doubts, in the confidence that you can get results for them. Under such conditions, you can often get answers to prayer, but you should encourage these people to realize that it was their faith in your call upon the God-power which enables it to work for them, and they could have accomplished the same result by direct communion with this God-power in their own minds.

A businessman came to visit me in New York. He needed to sell a piece of real estate which he had put on the market in his home state of Illinois. His wife was facing an operation and he had to convert this property, as soon as possible, into cash. A real estate agency, which he had employed to make the sale, had just written him that they saw little hope of disposing of the house and lot at the present time. This man said to me, "If *they* can't sell it—and they are right on the ground, with all possible contacts—how can I?"

"Are you going to accept the negative attitude of this real estate company?" I asked. "Are you going to let your fears that you can't sell it fill your mind so that you can't see anything else? If you do you will never sell the property. You will demagnetize all possible interest in it from the minds of any persons who might be looking for just such a place."

"You mean to tell me," said this man, "that if I can free my mind of the fears I have that this property can't be sold—and that if I can picture people who are looking for property like mine, finding it and buying it—that this place can be sold?"

"That is exactly right," I insisted. "If you can have that faith, if you can picture that happening in your mind's eye, and if you can pray to the God-power within you and ask this Power to put the forces into motion to bring this to pass—it will happen!"

"Sounds absolutely fantastic," said the man, "but my need is so great I'll try anything!"

"Its not as easy as that," I cautioned. "You can't *make* yourself believe just because you want an answer to prayer. You can't kid the God-power. You must genuinely believe that what you are praying for can and will come to pass; otherwise nothing will take place. You will be just going through the motions. It won't mean anything."

"Suppose *you* visualize for me," proposed this man. "You've had experience with this God-power. It's worked for you, but it hasn't for me."

"Oh, yes, it has," I pointed out, "whether you have realized it or not. Every time you have had a strong desire for something and had faith that you would and could get it—and have finally achieved it—you have actually been praying for it, and the God-power within has helped you get an answer to prayer. You may not consciously have prayed, but you have performed the technique of prayer and have gotten the result you pictured. Nothing can ever come to you, good or bad, that you have not attracted to you by right or wrong thinking."

This was a new thought to this man—a thought which gave him a jolt.

"You see," I added, "you cannot get away from this God-power. It is a part of your consciousness. God does not compel you to use it rightly. You can get it to serve you constructively only if you so direct it by your right thinking. You are a creature of free will and free choice. You must free your mind of destructive feelings and make yourself receptive before you can receive good things in answer to the right kind of desires—and prayers. Quite often people pray for the wrong kind of things because they are dominated by the wrong desires. God doesn't stop you when you want something that is not right or good for you. He lets you punish yourself by the unhappy experiences you bring upon yourself. He knows that in time you will learn how to operate so that you can improve your conditions in life. It is the only way you can gain any lasting happiness, health, prosperity, or peace of mind."

We finished our meditation and prayer together. Late the following day, this man phoned me in a state of high elation.

"It's happened!" he reported. "I just got a long-distance call from an old friend of mine. He said he had sold his home and was looking for a smaller place to live, since he had only his wife and himself left, with his children married and in homes of their own. Last night, as he was talking with his wife about possible places in town, both of them hit on my place and wondered, since I had been away so many years, if I might be interested in selling. They decided to find out where I was and phone me, and we made a deal. It's absolutely unbelievable!"

This man got his answer almost immediately, but you shouldn't wait until you or your loved ones are confronted by an apparently insurmountable problem before resorting consciously to prayer. The time to start practicing prayer for yourself or others is now. If you can get recognizable results in small things, you can get them as effectively when big things are needed, provided you can control your fears and worries, and see clear, confident pictures of what you want, and hold these pictures, with faith, until they are brought to pass.

V

Specific Prayers for Specific Needs

During the past thirty years, thousands of men and women have written to me, seeking an answer to their personal problems. In my extensive travels about the country, lecturing and presenting classes in self-development, I have talked to thousands more.

In every case, I have sought to impress each person, however great his need, that the answer exists within himself. I have explained verbally, and in books on the functioning of mind and emotions, that a part of God, the Great Intelligence, dwells in each of us. I have emphasized that when we learn to draw upon the God-given creative power within, through right visualization and the right approach to God—in prayer—we can find the right solution to all problems.

It weakens you if I give you my opinion of what you should do; it strengthens you if I show you how you can decide yourself what is the best procedure to meet one of life's problems. You want to be able to stand upon your own feet, to get results for yourself. You want to know where your thinking may have been wrong, so you can correct it and avoid unintentionally creating more trouble for yourself in the future. But depending on someone else to solve your problems is unwise. You will never develop self-confidence and faith and assurance in that manner.

A friend or loved one can pray *for* you or *with* you, but if you would derive permanent benefits from this you must go direct to God, in prayer, and be willing to expend whatever effort is necessary to help realize what you need or desire.

Quite often, however, it is difficult for you to put in words the attitude of mind you wish to achieve or the things you wish to attract to you.

Many men and women have said to me: "I just don't know how to be specific when I pray. For instance, I need to make my consciousness receptive to receive guidance from this God-center in me." Or "I need to develop the ability to adapt myself to others." Or "I need to acquire more patience and tolerance and understanding." Or "I need to learn how to activate the healing power in my mind so I can overcome injuries and illness." Or "I need to know how to pray so that I can operate the law of abundance and help solve my financial problems." Or "I need to be able to relax my body and my mind so that I can attune myself to the God Presence." Or "I need to improve the expression of my personality through right thinking and prayer." Or "I need to be capable of attracting the right life companion to me." Or "I need to get a deeper feeling of kinship with all races of people."

These are all basic needs which require specific prayers in order to impress the God-power within and cause it to bring about changes in your consciousness which will, in turn, attract what you desire to you.

In answer to these needs, I prepared eight specific prayers, and presented them to the students in my classes from coast to coast. They repeated these prayers, as a group and individually, in the privacy of their own homes, making them a part of their own minds and hearts. Many reported phenomenal results, great and gratifying changes in their lives and in the nature and quality of their thinking and their feeling.

Keep in mind that each of these prayers has been tested by human experience. Each has been used by other men and women like yourself, made a part of their consciousness and thus a part of their lives. Each has brought the results desired as these people have given deep thought to its meaning and have repeated the words with sincere and heartfelt feeling.

Unless you accept a thought or an idea—even in the form of a prayer—it cannot become manifest in your life. These specific prayers will serve you only to the degree that you put your own faith and need behind them.

Every fundamental need is covered, specifically, in the following eight prayers:

1. Prayer for Inspiration
2. Prayer for Adjustment
3. Prayer for Re-Creation
4. Prayer for Abundance
5. Prayer for Attunement
6. Prayer for Personality Expression
7. Prayer for Companionship
8. Prayer for Brotherhood

You will notice, as you study these prayers, that the first part of each prayer enables you to prepare your mind to receive that for which you are praying. Too often, without any meditative preparation, we offer up a prayer before the mind is given an intelligent, concise picture of what we want. Then we wonder why the prayer is not answered. If you give a child scant or general instructions of something you want him to do, you cannot expect him to carry out your wishes satisfactorily.

These prayers are designed to help you attain what you desire and deserve. You can do this by setting aside a certain time, preferably the first thing in the morning and the last thing before retiring at night, and sitting quietly and repeating each prayer, over and over, as you feel the need, until it becomes *your* prayer—a living part of your own mind and heart. You must believe that what you desire, as expressed in prayer, you not only deserve but have the power to receive. This faith must be positive, expectant, unwavering. Your prayer will not be answered unless you pray with utter sincerity, unselfishness, simplicity, and directness.

As you repeat these prayers, you will find

that they will help you get into the mood to pray, that they will arouse in you the desire to achieve that for which you are praying, and that you can begin to feel the God Presence within as you pray.

In this way, God will become personal to you, and as you maintain your awareness of His Power within, this increasing feeling of personal kinship with God will grow. You will never again feel alone or without guidance and protection. You can turn to God in prayer whenever you feel the need, and you will realize that true prayer is far more than a mere petition to God to do everything for you without any effort or responsibility on your part. It is a dedication of your entire being, expressed through faith in yourself as well as in God.

Select the prayer for which you feel a specific need at the moment, and let it speak for you as you speak it. These prayers, repeated thoughtfully, with great sincerity of purpose, and with feeling, will eventually bring about such a change in your own consciousness as to change for the better every phase of your life. Unless you have a clear picture in your mind and in your heart of that for which you are praying, you cannot put real feeling or intelligence behind it.

Give your full attention to each line of each prayer. It is packed with meaning and substance. There is not a superfluous word. Each word is there for a purpose. And each time you address God as "Our Father" and use the word "I" it is intended that you establish a feeling of relationship between you and your Creator.

The prayers do not require any interpretation. They explain themselves. They need only the full identification of your own self with them to take on the power that is in them. You, your faith, and your desire for self-development and attainment are the generators of that power. The answers you want are waiting only your conscientious application of these prayers to your own needs.

Do not memorize them. You can put these same thoughts in your own words if it is more natural for you to express them this way.

Prayer for Inspiration

Our Father,
Eternal source of all power and wisdom and intelligence,
Help me to prepare my mind so that I can

receive
From Your indwelling presence
The knowledge and guidance I need
To live a happy, successful life.
Help me to understand that, as a creature of
Free will and free choice,
I am never compelled but am always offered
The opportunity to follow your guidance.
Help me to remember that this guidance
May come to me in the form of inner urges,
Impulses, impressions, feelings, and ideas,
And that, through what I call intuition,
You answer prayer.
Help me, at all times, to recognize the difference
Between wrong and right thinking, feeling, and action.
Help me to know that,
As I pray with faith,
In full willingness to put forth every effort
Toward attainment on my part,
Your power within will attract to me
The resources and circumstances and even the people I need,
To make that for which I have prayed come to pass.
Realizing all this, dear Father,
In full faith, I now pray

That the channels of my mind will always be
open
To receive inspiration and guidance and
protection
From Your indwelling presence.
Amen

Prayer for Adjustment

Our Father,
Creator of all people,
Help me to see
In them, aside from all seeming differences,
What I see in myself:
The same basic feelings and desires,
The same dreams and ambitions,
The same love of home and family,
The same inexpressible urge for a deeper
Understanding of self,
And a knowledge of God and the universe.
Help me to realize
That, however high or low in the scale of
Development my fellow humans may be,
I bear a kinship to them, of whatever race and
color,
As children of the same Creator.
Help me, therefore, to sense
The harm I am doing to myself when I permit

Prejudices against any race or individual to
Continue to exist in my mind and heart.
Help me to be forgiving
Of the failings of my human brothers,
As I would wish them to forgive me for my shortcomings.
Let me resolve, as I discover these shortcomings,
To do my best to change them,
As a first step toward inviting a similar change in others.
To this end,
I pray for the strength, the patience,
The understanding, and the will
To carry me forward each day in the service
Of my fellow humans,
So that I may do my share toward creating
A finer, happier life for myself and my dear ones.

Amen

Prayer for Re-Creation

Our Father,
Designer and Creator of the body in which I dwell,
In and through which I live and move and have my being,

Help me to realize
That the perfect pattern of my body is
contained in my mind,
That anything less than perfect which has
manifested
Or does manifest in this body
Has been the result of wrong thinking and
wrong
Operation of Your universal laws.
Should my body have been imperfect at birth,
It has still been the result of human
causations
And not by any divine decree.
Help me to realize
That Your creative power, which fashioned
this body,
Is still resident in my mind, ready to serve me
At any time of need;
That I, as a creature of free will, now have
control
Of this creative power,
And may direct it for my own good or ill,
Dependent upon the nature and character of
my thoughts
And feelings.
In full realization of this,
I now call upon Your creative power within
me

To correct and eliminate any and all body
imperfections.
As I do so,
I know that re-creation is taking place
In every cell and nerve and gland and tissue
and organ,
In direct accordance with the degree of my
vision and my faith.

Amen

Prayer for Abundance

Our Father,
Eternal source of all supply,
Help me to realize
That there is no lack in any needed resource,
At any time or in any place,
Except as I create that lack through my own
Wrong or limited thinking.
Help me to fix in my mind
The assurance that there is an answer to my
every need
Through Your creative power which resides
in my consciousness.
Help me to remember that this creative
power
Responds to my fears and desires . . .

That it will attract to me exactly what I picture in my mind.
If I picture lack—I will get lack,
And if I picture plenty—I will receive plenty.
Help me to develop an attitude of mind which
Pictures gain instead of loss,
Success instead of failure,
And which profits from every experience, good or bad.
Thank You, dear Father, for the law of abundance,
Which I may call upon through prayer
To supply me whatever I need at any time.
Help me now to assume and maintain
The constant awareness that I possess within me
The power to meet all my material needs,
And that I will not lack for any good thing from this moment on.

Amen

Prayer for Attunement

Our Father,
Whose Power resides within me,
Of whose consciousness I am a part,
In whom I move and have my being—
Help me to know that

You, my Creator,
Have instilled in me the power and the wisdom
To create for myself the world in which I live,
To deliver myself from the evil of my own wrong thinking,
To lift myself from where I am to where I wish to be
By releasing all feelings of fear and resentment and hate,
By forgiving others as I would be forgiven,
And by keeping myself in attunement with Your indwelling presence.
I thank You, dear Father,
For the inner assurance that I am never alone,
That You are always with me,
And that I may turn to You for guidance and protection
Whenever I feel the need—
For You are the power and the wisdom and the love
That will abide with me forever.

Amen

Prayer for Personality Expression

Our Father,

Giver of the priceless gift of my personality,
Help me to realize that my personality,
Different from that of any other creature
In all Your vast domain,
Is the outward expresison of my soul, my real self.
Help me to know that there is no inequality in personality,
That my personality has the same value,
The same potential worth,
The same eternal promise of development
As that of any soul, any time, anywhere
In Your great universal scheme of things.
Help me to be increasingly aware
That my personality is my exclusive and eternal possession,
To develop and express as I choose.
Help me to remember that, as I demonstrate
A sincere and helpful interest in others,
Just so does my personality become more magnetic and appealing.
Grant, therefore, dear Father,
That I possess the resolution to give thought, each day,
To the fuller expression of my personality,
In mind and act,
That I may overcome all feelings
Of fear, inferiority, self-consciousness,

And dislike for any person or thing.
As I am able to do this, dear Father,
I know that I will be expressing Your spirit and Your plan for me,
Through this, my unfolding personality.
Amen

Prayer for Companionship

Our Father,
Eternal Indweller of all life whose presence I feel within me,
Help me to find a loving, understanding companion,
The man or woman I need to make my life complete on this earth,
Either as a friend or as a mate.
Help me to realize
That my power to attract such a companion depends upon me,
How acceptable I am able to make myself
In appearance, in personality, in character,
In a sincere, unselfish interest in others.
Help me to know that there is someone seeking me
As earnestly as I am seeking that someone.
Help me to have faith that the love and companionship

For which I yearn is within my reach.
Help me, dear Father, to put aside my feelings of loneliness,
And to look forward, with faith and expectation,
To the making of new friends and associations.
Help me to remember that I must be a friend
To have a friend . . . that I must love to beget love.
From this moment on, I promise to do my part.
I will open my mind and heart and send out the call
For that someone I need.
I do this in the faith that this prayer has been heard
And is even now answered.
And I thank You, dear Father,
For the evidence of Your unfailing love and companionship,
Which always sustains me.
Amen

Prayer for Brotherhood

Our Father,
In whose consciousness there is naught but

Love and peace and harmony,
Help me fill my own mind with
Love, peace, and harmony,
As I declare now my belief in You
And in others.
Help me, O Father, to make secure this belief
In my mind,
To make it so much a part of me that I begin
    living it
In my daily contact with others—my
    brothers and sisters.
Grant that there be given to me
The tolerance and the understanding and the
    forgiveness
To love my brothers and sisters though
    mindful of their failings,
Ever mindful, too, of the failings that are
    mine,
Which I am striving each day to overcome.
Strengthen, therefore, my belief in You,
And in others, as I give expression to this
Belief in these words:
I believe—
In one God, Father of all.
In one humanity, every man my brother,
    every woman my sister,
In one common freedom of thought and
    expression

Established among all races and nations.
In one world of unity and cooperation.
In one purpose—mutual love and
understanding.
And in this to the end that all may attain
One great goal in life—universal peace and
happiness.

Amen

VI

Prayers for a Small Child

Today, our children are ushered into a world which is changing so fast that most adults have difficulty keeping pace with it. Young minds are filled with impressions received from a barrage of magazines, picture books, motion pictures, radio and television programs, what is taught at school and what is picked up at home and at play.

It is almost impossible to protect the mind of a child from exposure to every manner of thought and idea, whether or not some of these thoughts and ideas are years ahead of the child; it is no wonder that the average child is precocious. Knowledge is increasing at a rapid rate, and small children often know more about sex than their elders knew until they had reached their late teens. As a child develops, there is added to his problems that of his attitude toward prayer, and his concept of God.

Some may still be led to believe in a God not too unlike an earthly parent who loves his children, who rewards them when they are good but punishes them when they disobey. This is a satisfying concept when the child's home life is happy and he is blessed with understanding, loving parents for whom the child can feel trust and love in return. But, if the child has come from a home where either parent has shown little regard or respect for the children, it is not easy for a child to accept God as a father or mother whom he can love and to whom he prays.

In these times it is perhaps wisest, nevertheless, to teach the small child that God is like a good parent who will listen to his troubles and help him when he needs help, if he will pray to God and tell God what he wants and how he feels about things. The child must have an image of God in his mind for whom he can develop a feeling of reality as well as personal contact.

God might be described as resembling a great central broadcasting station—He is everywhere at once, and anyone who wishes may talk to Him and pray to Him whenever the need is felt. God cannot be seen, but a child may know He is present and that He hears everyone's prayers because He always answers them if the prayers are for something good.

But a child may ask, "What is good?" and this concept of "good" may be as difficult to get across as the concept of God. Actually, the spirit of God and the spirit of good are closely allied. Good may be said to be the expression of God in life.

To convey this idea to the mind of a small child requires a simple approach, with words which have meaning to a child, as well as feeling. Unless a child can feel the effects of a good act growing out of a good thought, he cannot develop any real comprehension or appreciation of it.

Here, then, is a series of statements which, read to the child or repeated by the child, establishes in his consciousness what "good" is in terms of his everyday experience:

God is how you feel when you feel good.
You feel good when you are helping
Mother and Daddy.
You feel good when you are smiling.

You feel good when you are singing.
You feel good when you are going to school.
You feel good when you are with your friends.
You feel good when you are clean.
You feel good when you are making someone happy.
You feel good when you are petting your dog or cat.
You feel good when you are feeding the birds.
You feel good when you are walking in the rain.
You feel good when you are playing in the snow.
You feel good when you are sitting in the sunshine.
You feel good when you go swimming.
You feel good when the wind pushes you.
You feel good when you are picking flowers.
You feel good when you are planting seeds.
You feel good when you are running.
You feel good when you are eating.
You feel good when you are resting.
You feel good when you are waking up.

You feel good when you are making
something.
You feel good when you are drawing
pictures.
You feel good when you are pretending
what you will be when you grow up.
You feel good when you are with your
playmates.
You feel good when you are thanking
God for all His goodness.
As long as you feel good, you are close to
God and God is close to you.

These are powerful associative suggestions and will help the child develop the right mental attitudes toward his daily activities and interests. When "good" comes to mean things that he likes or likes to do, he will look forward to them and strive to *be* good and *do* good because of the good feeling engendered.

A child can be reached through feeling when reason does not, as yet, persuade. He should always be approached on his level and never "talked down to." A child is inherently good, and this urge to be good should be capitalized upon by placing emphasis upon what is good, rather than accentuating the bad every time he makes a mistake. Otherwise, he may get the idea that what is characterized as bad—what he is forbidden to do—may be more pleasurable and exciting than the so-called good things.

If a child can see God, as well as goodness, in the world about him, he will respond to his varied experiences in a positive, constructive way. The following statements, either read to the child or repeated by the child, will aid him in reacting as he should to the world as he finds it, and to sense the presence of God in his world. These statements will answer, more understandably for the child, the question, "What is God?"

You cannot see God, but God is all
    around you, all the time.
God is everywhere, and everything is a
    part of God.
God made the sun that shines by day.
God made the moon that shines by night.
God made the stars in the heavens.
God made the earth on which you live.
God made the sea.
God made the mountains.
God made the trees.
God made the winds that blow.
God made the rains that fall.

God made the birds that fly.
God made the flowers that grow.
God made the ground beneath your feet.
God made the rocks.
God made the fish.
God made the animals.
God made your body—the house in
 which you live.
God made your eyes that see.
God made your ears that hear.
God made your tongue that tastes.
God made the air your breathe.
God made the water you drink.
God made the food you eat.
God made everything.
God made you and listens to you when
 you pray.
God protects you from harm.
God helps you when you want something
 that is good for you.
God loves you, as your father and mother
 love you,
because you are one of God's children.

When a child can be led to picture God in nature, he can then begin to personalize a feeling for God. As the child matures with this concept, he gains a greater awareness that a part of God, the Great Intelligence, actually dwells within his consciousness. He sees, increasingly, the evidence of God without him—and *feels* the presence of this God-power *within.*

Prayer, to a child so reared, becomes real and vital. He does not have to be brought back to God at a later age, through prayer, by punishing life experiences. He travels the path of life with God as his companion, calling constantly upon Him for guidance and protection.

A most remarkable concept of God was written by a fourteen-year-old girl, Charlene Bliss, of Arlington, Virginia, when her Sunday school teacher gave her pupils the assignment to write a short essay on the subject, "What is God?" This is what Charlene wrote:

What is God—or is there a God? What does He look like? Is He a man or an image? Is He an idea which man has developed to meet his needs? What do you *think? What do* you *believe?*

To me, God is not something you can point to and say, "There He is." God isn't something you can paint a picture of—unless you paint a picture of all the flowers, all the birds, all the living beings, and all the love in the world today.

I believe that God is an idea—a creative being which forces the flowers from their buds, holds the birds up in the sky, and pushes us on and on into a better world.

God isn't a miracle man to whom we can go with our problems, and say, "Please, God help me!" God helps those who help themselves. If we have faith in ourselves, as well as in our own idea of God, we have built a wall within ourselves that will never fall.

But you say, "Have faith in what? How can I believe? What can I believe?"

Through many experiences you will develop your own idea of God. Listen to what others have to say, and form all the ideas into one idea—your idea of God.

Here from the mind of one we would still consider a child, is one of the most inspired concepts of God. Charlene Bliss is an unusually sensitive, intelligent young lady. She would have to be, to have such perceptions—but her enlightened concept of God demonstrates the advanced thinking of many of our young people today.

Many adults who have become lost and

confused, mentally and emotionally, should try a childlike approach to God. If you are one of them, repeat these statements to yourself while you let their full meaning take possession of you. The greatest truths may be couched in the simplest language, although the modern tendency is to define God and the cosmos in terms so complicated that the average person cannot grasp it.

There is nothing complicated about genuine faith. It is the "*knowing* feeling" that what is desired is going to come to pass, with God's help.

When a child has belief, it is a whole-hearted, unquestioning belief. For this reason no promise should be made to a child unless it can and will be kept. To break faith with a child is to shatter his trusting nature. Each prayer a child says must be intelligible to him for him to have faith in it.

One of the most common of childhood prayers is the familiar:

Now I lay me down to sleep,
I pray the Lord my soul to keep;
If I should die before I wake,
I pray the Lord my soul to take.
Amen

It is doubtful if any child really understands this prayer, simply worded though it is. Death is difficult enough for an adult to comprehend, and a child, ordinarily far removed from death in the vibrancy of life, cannot imagine what it means to die.

I have heard children, my own included, recite this prayer and others like it, with double-time speed, so that they can get it over with as quickly as possible and be ready for the bedtime story.

It may amuse some parents to watch their offspring kneeling by their beds and delivering these prayers as so many words, without any thought or feeling concerning them. But something more substantial is needed if the child's mind is to be channeled into right thinking at an early age.

Eddie Rickenbacker and many other men and women have testified that they "learned to pray at their mother's knee." It is safe to say that these mothers took the moment of prayer seriously and that they impressed such moments on their children. Quite often parents get down on their knees beside their children, inspiring deeper respect and reverence for God; but other parents achieve the same result by having their children pray after they have gotten into bed. There is no specific posture; the best is the one that seems natural and right.

There is one rule in the creation and provision of prayers for small children: *keep them simple and keep them brief.*

The nightly prayer should apply to members of the family as well as to the child so that he is taught to think of himself in relation to others, and to request God's help not just for himself but for all in his family group. For instance, such a prayer might be: "Please, God, take care of Mommy and Daddy and Sis and Grandma and me . . . and help me, every day, to be a better boy (or girl). Amen."

Here you have a prayer that takes the family into account and also makes the child think of himself and his conduct. These are good thoughts to carry over into sleep, because we now know that the God-given creative power works while we sleep, and much good is accomplished for the individual, on subconscious levels, during sleep. Expressing a desire to be helped to be a better boy or girl stimulates action in consciousness and establishes a powerful pattern for good conduct in the mind of the maturing child.

Not too much thought is given to prayer for the small child, because few adults realize the possibilities of mind development in the young, and the influence of simple, meaningful prayers on a child's conduct and achievement. This is a field for exploration and expansion. A child can be encouraged to help himself in many ways by giving him prayers which possess a powerful suggestive value.

Consider a child who is plagued by stuttering. First, discover the emotional cause as soon as possible and eliminate it, and also have him say something like this each night: "Please, God, when I wake up in the morning, let me speak as well as anyone else."

Stuttering is usually brought on by feelings of inferiority and self-consciousness. The child feels he is not as good as someone else, he feels overshadowed, overwhelmed, incapable of properly expressing himself. His inner desire is to do as well as other members of the family. He naturally wants to speak as well as anyone else, and he can—the instant he thinks he can—unless there is a physical impediment, which does not exist in the majority of cases. The child can be encouraged to make up his own prayer along these lines, putting it into his own words. Once he gains emotional control, his troubles are over. If he develops the faith that he can do it, with God's help, he will recover his ability to speak clearly and without hesitation.

Many difficulties and bad habits in the life of a child can be removed or relieved by praying quietly beside the bed of the sleeping child.

Apply the technique of suggestive praying to whatever needs exist. If you persist, with faith, you are certain to get results. But you cannot and must not attempt to use mental force. The child's mind will resist unless you give it opportunity to cooperate of its own free will on this subconscious level.

Some children have been taught to pray more as a duty or a ritual. The parents pay little attention to the ceremony, although they make the usual nightly checkup.

"Have you said your prayers yet?"

If the answer is "No, Mommy," the reply is, "Well, hurry up and say your prayers and go to sleep!"

It is no wonder that one little boy finally rebelled against this kind of procedure and remarked one night, "Mommy, I'm not gonna pray tonight. I'm gonna take a chance!"

The prayer for "insurance" is a good prayer if it is sincerely meant; but insincerity always registers on the inner consciousness when you pray, and God is not fooled. He knows whether or not you are in earnest, and He acts in your behalf only when you impress Him that you really want an answer to your needs. A child can enjoy as close a contact with the God-power through prayer as an adult. His faith can be equally as strong, if not stronger—and a child's belief that God will hear his prayer and act upon it can produce astonishingly quick, positive results.

Parents have sometimes asked their children to pray for help when they have been so ridden by fears and worries that they could not pray effectively for themselves.

In time of family crisis, it is well to confide in the children, explain the problem to them as simply as possible, and invite them to join you in prayer. The fervent, sincere prayers of children, added to your own, can be of great aid. This enables you to unite the power of faith of all concerned, a strong sympathetic bond of feeling is created, and when the God-power is reached and activated under these conditions, things begin to improve.

A child's interest in prayer is greatly heightened when he hears his father and mother pray, and sees and knows their faith in prayer. You do not have to make a public display of it. Some children have been embarrased by their parent's bowing their heads and praying audibly in public restaurants.

True prayer is the means of communicating directly with the God-power within. For individual and family purposes, it should be kept personal and intimate. When a child is old enough, he should be encouraged to put his prayers into his own words so he can talk to God as he chooses and make known his needs in his own way. Prayers by the child then grow into prayers by the maturing young man and woman who have learned to rely upon God for guidance in all things, and, as a consequence, are living happy, healthy, self-assured lives. When and if this happens, your fondest prayers for your children will have been realized.

VII

How to Reestablish Faith in Prayer

A disillusioning experience can destroy, for a time, your faith in prayer.

E.C. was a beautiful, highly talented woman, a composer and an organist in a New England church, a private music instructor, active in community affairs, married to one of the leading attorneys of the town. To all appearances, J. and E.C. were one of the happiest couples in their set, and they were always on the go—too busy, they confessed, to take time out for children, much as they would like to have had them.

Much of E.'s time was taken up with various church activities in addition to her musical contributions. She considered herself to be a deeply religious person. But when she came suddenly upon unmistakable evidence that her husband had been having an affair with his secretary, the shock almost killed her. She had known for some time that he had been drinking excessively, but she had ascribed it to their high-pressure living. It was unthinkable to her that her husband could and would be unfaithful.

Her first impulse was to get away from it all, to seek refuge from her crushed feelings in flight. And so, in her desperation, she wrote to me, having read my book, *Your Key to Happiness.* She asked me if she might come to see me in California, where I was then living.

"I can't understand why this had to happen to me," she said when I saw her. "I have always lived a good, Christian life. I thought I had everything any woman would want—a good husband, a good home, a good name in the community. And then, overnight, it is all gone! If there's a God in heaven, why does He let me suffer like this? I can't pray anymore; I've lost all interest in music; I never want to see the inside of a church again. I can't look any of my friends in the face, and I won't ever go back to my husband. I don't see any reason for living!"

"Then why did you travel three thousand

miles to see me?" I asked. "Why didn't you end it all back east and save yourself this time and expense?"

She looked at me for a moment; then she smiled faintly and said she guessed she still did want to live, despite everything that had happened, if she could only find some way to put her broken life together once more.

I explained that this complete revulsion was a natural reaction in an experience like hers, and that it would take time for her to adjust herself, emotionally and mentally, to what had happened. I then suggested that she should locate somewhere in California for a few weeks and let herself feel that she had come out on a vacation, and give her mind and emotions a chance to be freed of their present agitation. In time, she could develop a new perspective and be able to work out a sensible solution to her problem.

She rented a room in a private home overlooking the ocean. She said she had made herself do this because no matter how hard she tried, she could not sleep at night, tortured by thoughts of her unhappy experience. I pointed out that she couldn't change what had happened and that she must get her mind off the past and give thought to the future which possessed the only possibilities for bringing new happiness.

"But I had the happiness I wanted once," she said. "I was satisfied with my way of life. If I can't have that happiness back, I don't want any!"

She was insistent about this, so I didn't attempt to argue with her. Feeling that her disturbed mental state would resist any proposals, I simply reminded her that she knew only too well that her present attitude would solve nothing and would only prolong and intensify her unhappiness.

The following day, in late afternoon, I received a long-distance telephone call from the woman's landlady to report that she had met with a serious accident. She had gone swimming, and a sudden wave had dashed her against a rock, causing a severe fracture of the right arm between the elbow and the shoulder. She had been taken to the nearest hospital, where X rays had revealed the severity of the break, and immediate surgery had been necessary to set the bones. The landlady said that the woman had requested that I be informed of the accident, and that she would appreciate my praying for her, since, as I knew, she couldn't pray for herself.

It was clear to me that her disturbed mental state had made her susceptible to this accident. She had pictured herself as having nothing more to do with music or the church, as not having any reason for living. The creative power within had taken her at her word. It had helped attract a mishap which had broken her arm so badly that she might not be able to play the organ again. Her career might definitely have been ended by her highly emotionalized visualization.

Her situation was further complicated by the fact that she was in no mood to attempt to help herself by trying to make contact with the God-power within. I knew that in her present emotional state she would look upon this latest misfortune as just more evidence that God was not interested in her or her welfare. This would make it difficult for the healing power within her mind and body to function effectively, and especially difficult for anyone seeking to help her, through prayer, to get any results.

In my prayers, I asked the God-power within her to let E.C. realize how much music had meant in her life, and to give to her the urge to want to recover the full use of her arm so she could play as well as ever, knowing that a change in her own consciousness was imperative if healing were to take place.

Two days later, I learned from the landlady that E.C. had requested she be sent back to her home, so that a famous bone surgeon in Boston could take over her case. The doctor who had operated on her arranged the flight himself, after placing her in a tight body cast. He then took her to the airport in his car and saw her safely aboard. This report indicated to me that she had recaptured a desire to live, and that she was still interested in her musical career.

Further surgery was required in Boston, and then a prolonged amount of physiotherapy. When she was able to use a typewriter, she pecked out letters to me, reporting her progress. She confessed that at first the accident had seemed to be the end, but then as she lay in the hospital under kind and efficient care, it suddenly came over her that the world was a pretty fine place after all, with a lot of fine people in it, and that, if necessary, she could establish a new life in a new community and find much to enjoy.

Back in her home state, attended by the surgeon whom she had known for many years, E.C. was visited by the minister of her church and some of her pupils, and friends who had journeyed to Boston to see her. They all expressed a heartwarming desire for her to return home, and told her how much they had missed her presence in the church, and her music. No one mentioned her unhappy marital upset, but she had learned from the minister that her husband had been in poor health and had appealed for help to the local Alcoholics Anonymous group. So far as the minister knew, he was no longer going with the other woman, who he had heard had left town.

One day, I received a letter from E.C. which made me extremely happy. She wrote: *You will be glad to learn that I have started praying again. But I am not praying for myself; I am praying for my husband. You know, Mr. Sherman, I thought I could never forgive him for what he did, or get over the hurt he caused me. But this hospital confinement has given me an opportunity to do a lot of thinking, and I can see now where I've been to blame as much as he, for what's happened. So, I'm praying each night that he will get the strength to overcome his drinking and that he will want to come back to me. Mr. Sherman, I have never wanted a prayer answered as much as this one. Do you think God will grant it?*

I answered her letter immediately, with the assurance that there was every possibility, now that she had cleared her mind and heart of all resentment, that she and her husband might certainly be able to resume their life together.

Within a month came another letter: *My husband called for me at the hospital—and took me home! With God's help, I am going to make him the finest wife in the world. I don't know when I was ever happier than I am now. What happened seems only like a bad dream. What else can I say, except that God showed His love for me through strangers, and that through their kindness I found my faith again. Not only are J. and I together once more, but the doctors say I will have the full use of my arm. I am planning a return to my music. But J. and I are reserving lots of time for each other. My only prayers now are prayers of gratitude!*

It is a strange but true fact that sometimes you have to find your way back to God through adversity, after losing contact with Him as the result of a tragic experience. Your faith is tested each day as you face different trials. When life is going smoothly it is easy to believe that "God's in His heaven: all's right with the world." But let something go wrong and put a strain upon your faith in prayer and in God's power to help you, and the whole picture may change—for a while.

Actually, many who lose faith in prayer have really wanted their own way most of the time. Sooner or later, such men and women run up against a situation which is not in accordance with God's will. When this happens, the God-power does not function for them as they would like, and they get upset about it.

E.C. didn't see why she, a Christian woman, should have been subjected to such a community scandal. God should have stepped in and prevented J. from being unfaithful. The least God might have done would be to keep the matter private. It was impossible for E.C. to realize at the time of the occurrence that sins of omission can be as devastating as sins of commission; that by her indifference to her husband's needs she had been a contributor to his infidelity.

She had a mistaken idea of virtue and of prayer. She had the wrong interpretation of the meaning of "good." She had the self-centered idea that all she had to do was pray that she be surrounded by good and that only good would come to her, and God would take care of the rest.

But God always works with the material that is presented to Him. As E.C., in her concentration upon her own activities, was neglecting her husband and causing him to seek elsewhere what he could not find at home, her prayers for a happy home life were unavailing. She had to offer God the sacrifice of the things she was doing wrong before God could help her get a good result.

When E.C.—after the catastrophe she largely brought upon herself—awakened to her own faults and resolved to correct them, her prayers took on real meaning. They came from her innermost being, they were deeply felt, and they reached the God-power within at once, magnetizing conditions around her and attracting to her just what she pictured.

God, during the trying time she rejected Him, was powerless to offer guidance and protection. It must be emphasized again and again that prayer is a two-way proposition. It has been said that "man proposes and God disposes," but God's disposition depends always upon the nature of our proposal. If we are self-seeking or demanding, God is not moved. His power functions only when we and God are in harmony; otherwise there is never a right answer to prayer.

When it has never been your practice to pray, when you have sought to live your life without prayer, having no belief in its power or your ability to reach the God consciousness, you have to accept a great deal on pure faith, in the beginning, that the act of prayer will produce results which you could not otherwise attain.

Agnostics have said to me, "I can accomplish the same things without prayer that you can with prayer. You are just deluding yourself that you are getting help from God. Faith in yourself is all you need."

Faith in oneself is a first step. This you must have to achieve success in any worthwhile effort. But one's faith in self, whether realized or not, is usually based upon faith in a higher power. You feel, in a moment of great need, that you can call upon what you may define as a "reserve." You exercise a stronger belief in what you think to be yourself, and this extra demand brings new energy, new ideas, new and greater assurance, and you rise to meet an emergency in a way you ordinarily could not. God's cooperation is so subtle that it is difficult to know just when your effort ends and God's help begins. You actually, in your heartfelt aspiration, reach up to God, and He figuratively takes your hand and gives you a lift. This is a form of prayer without words. You have pictured fervently what you want and have sought mightily to get it—and then you have found a new area of power and attainment. Remain an agnostic, if you will; assume all the credit. But God was there in those moments and gave you the help of His power.

The God-given creative power within you is a limitless reservoir. No one has ever begun to tap its potential capacity. There is always more power available to the degree that any human learns how to draw upon it. This is the point in human consciousness wherein the individual soul touches infinity from the finite side.

A friend we will call C.N., who did not believe in the power of prayer but who had respect for me and my own belief, wrote me a letter from New York, saying he was in a desperate state of mind. He had lost his position with a book publisher some weeks before, and had not been able to make a new connection.

He was a translator of Latin and Greek manuscripts, specialized work for which there was not too great a demand. "I can't see anything ahead for me," he said in his letter. "My wife and I are near starvation and eviction, as I have been able to save nothing on the small salary I had been receiving. What can we do? And don't tell me to *pray!*"

I answered: "Change your picture. Stop seeing yourself out of work in your mind's eye. See yourself happily and busily at work in a new translating assignment with another publisher, receiving a better salary than before. Somewhere in New York—right now, this instant—there is a publisher looking for someone with your specific qualifications, just as earnestly as you are looking for that publisher. You must believe this to be true. Other translations are being done, despite the fact this is a limited field; and translators will always be needed. The only problem is to prepare your mind so that the God-power within can make the connection for you, and so magnetize conditions about you that you will be led to meet the right people, or that people you already know will think of you and recommend you to the publisher who needs your services. There are many ways that this higher power of your mind functions to aid you, when it is properly directed.

"I know this will be completely alien to your experience, but I *am* going to tell you to try prayer! I feel certain that prayer will place you in the right state of mind to attract new and better conditions.

"When you acknowledge the existence of a higher power, accept on faith that this power of God dwells in your own consciousness, and then start looking to God for help, you will instantly take the strain off your own body and mind.

"You are already, by your own admission, in a desperate state. You have exhausted every human possibility and tried every way you know to get a new job. Now, instead of picturing complete failure, a dead-end street, why not turn to God? You cannot get any light in your home, even though there is power in the wires, until you turn on the switch. May I suggest that you give prayer a trial: turn on the switch by picturing your need and asking the God-power within to help you. If you decide to do this, I will do what I can for you and with you during my periods of meditation and prayer."

C.N. fired a special delivery letter back:

"You win! We're giving prayer a week's trial, and we're putting everything we've got behind it. It will help us if we know you are praying with us."

I replied at once: "I'm glad you've made this decision. But let me warn you, if you pray with a disturbed mind, it will keep your prayer from reaching and impressing the God-power within, and will cause wrong conditions to happen instead. Throw out all your fears and worries. If you cannot develop sufficient faith in this God-power at the start, have faith in my own assurance that it will work for you. But you must believe, without forcing, that your prayer will be answered. If you will do this and persist, you will positively get the result you desire in time to meet your needs, however desperate they appear at the moment."

They followed this counsel. It took them a day to clear their minds of their fears. They then began to pray, thanking God for the new opportunity He had opened up to them, for the new publisher who had offered the new position, for the larger salary that had gone with the job. On the third day, a telegram was delivered to C.N., requesting that he contact a certain editor with one of the biggest New York publishers. This editor told him that he had phoned several publishers in search of a man of his abilities, and that C.N. had been strongly recommended by the house which had had to let him go. He was given one of the best assignments of his career, paying the highest salary he had ever received.

If you need to reestablish prayer in your own life or to seriously try prayer for the first time, you now know how to go about it. The results are waiting only upon your exercise of faith and your call upon God.

VIII

Health Through Prayer

Doctors agree that the mental attitude of a patient who is suffering from any serious illness or injury is most important. Many patients have died from shock or from fear, from lack of faith in their recovery, or the actual belief that they would not survive. All the efforts of medical science could not save these people.

"They have the will to die instead of the will to live," one doctor commented to me. "If I find a patient has little or no faith in God, I try to get him to have faith in me and in my ability to help make him well. Of course no doctor really ever cures a patient. He simply does what is necessary, through medication or surgery, to correct a condition sufficiently so that nature can finish the job.

"I have sewed up many bad wounds, but I didn't cause those layers of skin and nerves and muscles to grow together again. That wonderful re-creative power was supplied by the body and mind of the patient. A good doctor is only a plumber who responds to a trouble call, finds out what is the matter, fixes it—and then gets out of the way!"

More and more, the influence of the mind on the body is being recognized and techniques of right thinking have been developed to enable disturbed men and women to eliminate any adverse feelings and thus contribute materially to their recovery.

You know you don't feel well when your mind and your emotions are upset. Each body cell is affected by the way you feel, and is given what might be described as a positive or a negative charge. When you are happy, your body reflects this happiness in a surge of new vitality; you are uplifted physically as well as mentally. When you are unhappy, the body just as quickly reflects your depression; it is as depressed as you are, lacking energy and initiative.

If a mere optimistic or pessimistic attitude can have this immediate influence upon the body, reason must tell you that deeply felt fear, worry, and other adverse emotional reactions can really raise havoc.

When Fred Stone, famous musical comedy star, crashed in his plane some years ago and broke almost every bone in his body, doctors said it was impossible for him to live, and that if he did live he would be hopelessly handicapped. But they hadn't reckoned on the tremendous spirit and faith that Fred Stone possessed.

"I'm going to get well!" he announced, when he regained consciousness and learned of his condition. "Not only that—I'm going to dance again!"

Day after day, prayerfully, fervently, determinedly, Fred Stone kept repeating this declaration. He pictured his badly broken legs and arms and ribs and shoulders and hips healing. He refused to accept the verdict of doctors who shook their heads in amazement as Fred clung to life, day after day, and his bones began to knit, and new vitality developed in his battered body.

His friend, Will Rogers, had opened for him in a new musical show on Broadway for which Fred had been rehearsing. Will didn't make any pretense at being a dancer, so when he would come to the spots in the show where

Fred was to have danced, he would say, "Now, here is the place where Fred intended to turn a backward somersault, or do a hop, skip, and a jump. You'll just have to imagine it, because I ain't gonna do it!"

Long, painful, tedious weeks and months followed, during which Fred fought his way out of tractions and plaster casts and wheelchairs, and got himself up on his feet with the use of a cane. The breaks in his ankle bones, doctors said, would absolutely prohibit his taking a dancing step. But Fred left the hospital, went to his home in Forest Hills, rigged up some apparatus in his gymnasium, and pulled and tugged at his mending bones to keep his body from getting stiff.

Finally there came a day when it was announced that Fred Stone was replacing Will Rogers in the show, and joining his daughter, Dorothy, as the costar. It was a night that old-time Broadwayites will never forget. They stood and cheered when their beloved Fred Stone made his entrance in a "cane dance" which he had originated for the occasion. He and Dorothy danced it as the audience applauded with tears of joy and admiration for the courage and spirit of this great performer. He had proved that seemingly hopeless injuries can be surmounted if you have sufficient faith and the will to live and get well. Fred later danced, of course, without his cane, but he retained the "cane dance" as one of the great novelty numbers of the show.

There is no question about it—it is not the doctors who saved Fred Stone. They set the bones and attended to the mechanics, but Fred would not have survived and he certainly would never have walked again—let alone danced—had it not been for his faith that he could and would recover, plus his unwavering determination to get well, which had activated the God-given creative power within him and caused it to perform this miraculous job of healing.

Take inventory of your own courage and faith. Would you have been able to stand up under similar injuries? Fred Stone had to do his part before God could help him. He told God what he wanted when he said, "I'm going to be well. I'm going to dance again." He didn't compromise. He didn't say, "I'm going to live, even if I'm handicapped for the rest of my life." He pictured a complete recovery, and that was just what he got. His triumph over the lack of faith in others that he would even survive is testimony that you should never give up, that you should face any situation with the resolution to do everything you can to overcome it, regardless of how hopeless it may seem at the moment.

N.J.S. had his back broken by a shell during the second World War. This had necessitated a series of operations. He had recently undergone another one and had been put in a cast from his chin to his knees. He appeared doomed to spend the rest of his life in bed, and considered himself lucky to be alive.

"Don't ask me to pray," he said to a minister friend. "If you want to pray for me, it's okay—but I've never prayed in my life. However, I believe in the power of mind. I'll cooperate with you every other way I can."

"All right," the minister agreed. "Then this is what I want you to do. This is April. You've told me that October twentieth is your wife's birthday. I want you to use your imagination and start picturing yourself well and out of the hospital by that date. I want you to see your back completely healed, see yourself getting up and walking, and being able to bend over and touch your hands to the floor!" N.J.S. looked up and laughed, "You're kidding!"

"No, I mean it! You keep on picturing this; and I have absolute faith that God will heal you and get you out of this hospital at the time you specify."

In September, N.J.S. was so much better that he asked permission to go home. As he was still in a cast, permission was refused. Exasperated, he got hold of a razor blade, cut himself loose from an overhead projector, and slit the cast in two. Looking like a Frankenstein, he got up and walked across the room and then back to his bed.

The doctors censored him for this action, but were astounded that he could walk. N.J.S. now kept after them and finally got an X ray taken of his spine. There was no scar—nothing on his back to indicate that he had been operated upon.

Three days before October twentieth, N.J.S. was still encased in a cast. He was so sure that he was now physically sound that he set up a clamor, "Get me out of this straight-jacket and let me out of the hospital. My wife's birthday's coming up on the twentieth, and I promised her I'd be home to help her celebrate."

The morning of the twentieth, doctors, expressing considerable misgivings, removed the cast. N. stood up, bent over, and placed the palms of both hands flat on the floor.

The minister in this story, in my estimation, did pioneering work in developing and demonstrating the power of prayer. Many other ministers as well as laymen have other similar results, but I have had first-hand observation of the prayer techniques used by this man and his wife, and feel that they are of such value that they are worthy of detailing in this book. There are occasions, they declare, when it is helpful if someone will act as a stand-in for the afflicted individual. They give the following example:

One day a friend phones to tell them he had learned that his mother, in a neighboring city, had suffered a severe heart attack. She was very ill and in considerable pain, despite all medications. The friend asked my friends to do what they could for her.

That night, in their meditation period, the minister asked his wife to "sit in" for the mother.

"Fix your mind upon her," he instructed, "and let me place my hands on you—and take her pain." They concentrated and prayed for a few minutes.

"Father, who is within us," the minister

said, "manifest Thyself through us. I am now feeling the pain that this mother is suffering. Release this pain and make her heart perfect."

The pain disappeared after a moment, and the minister said, "Thank You, Father, for Your healing presence, and for restoring this mother to health."

Following the meditation period, they reported to the friend that they felt God had heard and answered their prayer. They asked him to write home and inquire if any change had occurred in the mother's condition. In several days they received a reply that, between the hours of ten and eleven of the night they had been praying, her pain suddenly left her, and a subsequent examination of the heart showed it to be functioning normally. She has not had another heart attack since.

It was not the words the minister used when he prayed, it was the feeling of conviction and of absolute faith that he put behind the words. He had such varied and successful experiences in the realm of prayer that he could almost instantly assume and maintain the right mental and emotional attitude when praying.

I asked him if it is necessary to perform a

"laying on of the hands" every time a healing prayer is offered. He said that it is not, although when it is convenient, physical contact may be more effective. The touch may mean much to an afflicted person, who is better able to picture a cure when he feels a hand upon the injured or afflicted area. "To some people, placing a hand upon their head, or different parts of the body, is like a benediction. It helps them get in the mood to join in prayer for their recovery. It is as though some kind of a circuit is closed between the two of us and the God-power within us. Once an individual really senses this, an instantaneous healing often takes place. They always testify that they feel much better, and progress usually then continues until they are well."

These people have not claimed that all of those seeking healing from them were healed. Individual obstructions of a physical or mental nature sometimes arose; but there is actually no limitation, in their opinion, when the healing power is activated. Seemingly hopeless cases do respond and recover when all else has failed.

It was interesting to me, as it will be to you, to learn approximately what the minister said when he treated for a healing through prayer. He told of a woman who came to him in acute pain from arthritis in her back, neck, and hands. He explained to her that her own emotions and past feelings had undoubtedly contributed to her condition, and that she would have to eliminate these feelings, as well as pray, if she hoped to be healed. The woman promised to do anything, to right any previous wrong, if only God would help her. The minister then asked her to be seated, and to relax in mind and body. He stood beside her and placed his hand first upon her head, as he prayed:

"Our omnipotent, omniscient, and omnipresent Father, we bring Mrs. S. into Your presence, to be treated by You, her Creator, in Jesus' name. I now speak my word to know that Your healing power is entering her body at this very moment, to relieve her of pain. (Here he touched the afflicted areas with his hands.) You are first taking away her pain, Father, that she may know You are present and manifesting. (Here the woman suddenly declared that her pain was gone.) I speak my word to know that Your healing power is now entering her heart, to cleanse it of all inner feeling of hate, resentment, and bitterness.

Your healing power is entering her subconscious life and taking from her the things which are hindering a perfect healing. And now, Father, I speak the word to know that Your healing power is now going into her arthritis and destroying the condition. Release her, Father, into thy healing love. It is done. Thank You, Father—thank You!"

"I often feel the healing take place myself," he related. "It may take the form of heat in the affected area, under my hands, or a vibration, or an electrical shock may strike me. The patient often feels this, too, and cries out about it. When a healing occurs, they know as soon as I know. When a pain I am sensing leaves me, it usually leaves them at the same time, during prayer."

"In this minister's opinion, which I share, the mere surface has been scratched in the achievement of healing through the power of prayer. I have related in my book, *Know Your Own Mind* (now out of print), a number of my own personal experiences wherein I was healed through faith in this God-given healing power and through prayer. On one occasion, I was healed of gangrene overnight, when the doctors had been prepared to amputate my foot the next morning.

So I can testify through many personal experiences that the accounts of healing in this chapter are true and not exaggerated, and that this God-power in you will serve you just as effectively as it has served me and countless others who have learned how to call upon it in times of great need.

Ernest Windle, who made a lifetime study of the influence of mind upon the body, during a discussion I had with him on the subject of prayer, suggested that, "Prayer triggers the glandular energies and pressures which, when oxidized, furnish the healing body chemicals in sufficient quantities to overcome infection and disease, as well as physical injuries."

Of course, something like this has to happen as a result of the prayer stimulation. I have said that when you pray for a healing, you *activate* the God-given creative power within. You picture, in your mind's eye, your body restored to health, and this becomes the blueprint the creative power goes to work on. It utilizes every function in the body to bring about the healing. It speeds up the action of glands and organs far beyond their so-called normal speed and efficiency of operation. Where instantaneous healings have taken place, such as at the famous town of Lourdes in France, time has been obliterated, and sores and swellings have shriveled and dried and disappeared before the astonished eyes of beholders.

There is a part of your subconscious which is not limited by your conscious concepts of time and space. When you reach this area of your mind with the right urge, in the form of a believing prayer, a higher power in you takes over.

In places like Lourdes, where many faith healings have been recorded, the very atmosphere is charged with the fervently felt faith thoughts of believers. When you enter this atmosphere and add your own faith to it you become attuned to it and get the benefit of it. Of course, quite a few seekers after health make trips to Lourdes and other faith centers, and are not helped. This is to be expected. God does not exist in any one place. He does not reside at Lourdes any more than He resides in your own home—in your own mind and heart. Your faith is not necessarily increased by a trip halfway around the world to a healing shrine—except that you might believe more strongly that you can be cured there. If your belief *is* intensified, then you do actually tune in on the powerful healing thoughts which have been generated by fellow humans, also in quest of renewed health, at such places as Lourdes. Then is when a so-called miracle occurs.

But "miracles," the operation of higher laws that we do not understand, can become manifest wherever you are, through the prayful intervention of a friend, or a prayer group, aided by your own prayers. If your faith in the healing power of God is sufficiently intense, your individual prayers will bring the desired result. Whatever brings you into genuine attunement with the God-power is all that is needed.

A pastor in Redbank, New Jersey, prayed in his regular Sunday morning service for the recovery of a parishioner who had been seriously injured in a train wreck and who was lying in a Perth Amboy hospital, still unconscious. He appealed to Jesus to go to this hospital, to walk up the stairs and down the hall to the room where this man was confined, giving the number of the room. He then, feelingly, said, "Now, Master, lay Your hand on his brow and heal him!" The congregation entered a moment of silent prayer following this plea.

At the hospital, doctors, who were ready to perform a brain operation, with the patient's pulse and respiration almost at the vanishing point, suddenly saw him open his eyes. He lapsed immediately into unconsciousness again. But when one of the physicians pinched him he reacted with a loud "Ouch!" The operation was called off, and it was only a few days before he had completely recovered. When a check was made as to the exact moment when the injured man had opened his eyes, it was found to have corresponded with the time that the minister and the congregation had prayed for him!

How are these miracles explained? Only on the basis that mind can communicate with mind—that the God-power in the consciousness of those who pray for others makes contact with the God-power in the consciousness of the ill or injured person.

You can regain your health through prayer. You can use the methods and techniques herein presented—or you can give expression to your physical and mental needs in your own words, in your own way. No one has a patent on an exclusive approach to God.

One man told me that he had prayed and prayed to be relieved of rheumatic pains, and nothing had happened. One night, he reached a point where it seemed that he just couldn't stand his affliction a minute longer, so he let out his pent-up feelings in a burst of profanity. He cursed the rheumatism, he cursed everything he could think of.

To his utter astonishment the pain disappeared, and has never returned! He then fell upon his knees and apologized to God for cursing. "But, God," he said as he concluded, "if you'd had this pain, I think you'd have cussed, too!"

Of course, what had really happened was this—he had never really meant his prayers before. He had never put genuine feeling into them. He had been too passive, too half-hearted. He hadn't actually believed that God would heal his rheumatism. When he finally realized that nothing was happening and probably wouldn't happen, his tremendously aroused desire to be healed activated the God-given creative power, and the rheumatism disappeared!

How *badly* do you want to be healed? How *deeply* do you believe you *can* be healed? How *willing* are you to put up a terrific fight, if necessary, to help the God-power within help you? Your answer to these questions will determine how quickly and completely your prayers are answered.

Don't leave it all up to God. Meet Him half-way, and you'll get results!

IX

Prayers in Business

When I was a young newspaper reporter in Marion, Indiana, I met a dynamic businessman who owned a chain of department stores. His name was Erle S. Kinnear, and he was far ahead of his time in the realization that a prayer service to start the day with all his employees would not only improve their outlook upon life, but give them increased sales ability.

I attended and spoke at some of those meetings which Mr. Kinnear, himself conducted. A large map of Grant County hung upon the wall behind the platform in the little store auditorium. This was the selling area which the Boston & Big Store served. Mr. Kinnear emphasized each morning that each sales clerk should carry in his or her consciousness the fact that the customers would honestly get greater values for less money in this store than any other store in the county. He reminded them that it was his policy to provide quality merchandise at a good price, and that they would undersell any other business to make good this policy.

"You must have real love in your heart for your customers," declared Mr. Kinnear, "and you must love to serve them. They must feel this sincere desire on your part to do what you can for them, to make them happy with the merchandise they buy."

This technique of right thinking was so comparatively new in those days that some of the employees privately thought Mr. Kinnear was a bit balmy, too religious, too given to fanciful, impractical operations. He told his employees if they had any family or personal problems, to come to him with them and he would try to help in the solution. He frankly stated that he had a selfish purpose in this, because he believed if any of his sales people had troubles on their mind, they could not do a good selling job, and it would be impossible to radiate a loving attitude.

Mr. Kinnear not only believed in the power of prayer, with which he ended every morning session just before opening time for the store, but he believed in the power of song. It was his conviction that men and women who sang in harmony would be better able to work in harmony. In line with this thinking, he appointed a song leader and had one of the women, an accomplished musician, at the piano. He even encouraged the development of a store chorus.

Townspeople were quite amused when they first heard of the "morning pep sessions" at the Boston & Big Store, and Mr. Kinnear was kidded about his new system of selling—loving the customers into buying goods from him—but nothing could dissuade him.

"You can't tell me that goodwill toward others won't pay off," he insisted. He was right.

The sales at the Boston & Big Store boomed, and folks in Grant County had to admit that God appeared to be on the side of Erle S. Kinnear. After a time, the employees began to observe that their own lives were becoming happier, that they were attracting better things to themselves, and they had to attribute this improvement to this new spiritual influence—the new philosophy of selling which their boss had given them.

The daily practice of thinking of the needs of the customer and trying to please the customer had rubbed off on these sales people and had made them more considerate of their friends and relatives.

"It's not easy to love a fault-finding, demanding, unreasonable customer," one of Kinnear's saleswomen said to me one day. "But I have tried to remember what Mr. Kinnear said to us—that every person has a part of God in him—and I do everything I can to overlook the cantankerous nature of the customer and appeal to the God side in him. I just know that if my God-power can reach his God-power I can bring out the better side. Perhaps the customer is depressed or mad or upset about something and feels that he has to take his feelings out on someone. If I should lose my temper too, as I used to do before I was taught to give out love to everyone, then I would only make matters worse. It may sound funny, but since I've used this kind of selling, I feel better physically and mentally, I enjoy my work more, the time goes faster, and I leave for home each night with a feeling that I've accomplished a lot more than just selling merchandise. I've given a lot of people a real lift by my cheerful attitude and sincere interest. Many now stop and tell me their troubles, sensing my sympathy, and when they get what is disturbing them off their minds, they buy even more than they had intended. Not only that, but they become regular customers. They like to return to a store where they know the sales people love to see them and love to serve them."

Of course, a sales program under the slogan of "Love That Customer" will not succeed unless it is carried through with genuine spirit. Insincere advertising, however well-worded, will not reach and impress the consciousness of the buying public for long. People's attention may be caught, but their buying power will not be held unless they get what they have been promised in goods and service.

In the 1930s, when my "Your Key to Happiness" radio program was conducted in New York City, I was invited to present an inspirational talk to the assembled employees of the Gimbel Brothers department store, at a morning meeting.

Mr. Flanagan, the then advertising manager of the store, was a great believer in the power of thought behind merchandising. He asked me to explain to the employees how they could draw upon their God-given creative powers to attract to them the things in life they most desired, and how to picture themselves improving their own sales abilities.

I stood upon a shoe bench in the shoe department on the fifth floor, surrounded by over seven hundred employees, and spoke to them for about twenty minutes. I told them how they could change their lives by picturing what they wanted through meditation and prayers each night before retiring. I suggested that they could practice the operation of these higher powers of mind, on their employers' time, at his expense, by picturing themselves making a sale to each customer. I gave them some of Erle Kinnear's technique. I pointed out that each customer is a law unto himself, that they would have to adapt themselves to different minds and temperaments in order to establish a harmonious relationship. I emphasized that, in the process of doing this, they would be developing the expression of their own personalities, learning how to get along better with their own friends and relatives, and would be increasing their own worth, not only to Gimbel Brothers, but to themselves. Then I stated that, as they became better salespeople and qualified to earn more money, they didn't need to be concerned about their future. If Gimbel Brothers didn't appreciate their increased value, some other firm was certain to recognize it—it is a law of life that you cannot give out without getting back—and you are paid back, always, if your thinking and your efforts are right, in the coin of your own giving.

The gong was ringing for the opening of the store just as I finished talking. Each employee was presented a copy of a pamphlet, then issued by my radio sponsors, titled, "Your Inner Key." They hurried off to their different departments and went to work.

The next morning, Mr. Flanagan called me and invited me to have lunch with him. I could tell that he was pleased and excited when we sat down together.

"Sherman," he said, "that was a terrific shot in the arm you gave our people yesterday. You'll be interested to know that they increased the sales record for that day by twenty percent over all previous years in the history of the store!"

This was not surprising to me because, when you harness the God-power within and commence making conscious, constant use of it, big things are sure to happen. These employees had an awakened desire to give better service, to test this God-given creative power to see if it really would produce results. When you want something badly, you are really praying for it, you are calling upon every power you possess, within and without, to get it.

Those who are using the God-power in business are using prayer, whether or not they pray openly or formally. But many heads of business and industry are starting their workdays with prayers today. Executives and foremen and employees will gather in separate groups or together, to give thought to God for a few minutes, before they take up their labors and the day's problems. In every instance where the prayer plan has been put into operation, there is proof that good had come from it.

In firms where no prayer service is held, top executives often bow their heads in silent prayer as they reach their desks, and ask humbly for guidance and strength to meet the day's demands.

God is entering the lives of more and more men and women in the business world. He is no longer remaining in church from Sunday to Sunday, when little thought or attention was paid to Him except for an hour or two of worship on the Lord's Day. He is going along with those who believe in His power as a constant companion and partner, giving counsel and courage to face problems as they arise.

It is heartening to realize that there is now a "prayer room" in the nation's Capitol where members of Congress, beset with all manner of pressures on important issues, may come and deliberate in silence, seeking, through an appeal to God in prayer, the right answer to problems affecting the country and the world.

In Washington, senators, congressmen, Supreme Court justices, businessmen, military leaders, men and women in various leadership classifications are attending different religious breakfast group meetings, where they can engage in a brief worship and prayer session and carry the inspiration of this communion with God into their responsible daily activities.

Go anywhere in the country, big cities or small, and you will find a steadily increasing number of community leaders who are seeking God's guidance in the management of their personal and business lives. The rank and file of the citizens are following this example, or are setting an example themselves through their own devotions.

This recognition of the power of prayer has come not so much from the churches and the different faiths, active as they have been in an encouragement of prayer functions, but the desire to retain closer attunement with God is emanating from the people themselves. All people, regardless of their religion can be united by prayer. When they pray together, expressing a common desire or need, God rewards them according to their faith and not in accordance with their denomination.

Fear of a possible third world war, with its unthinkable devastation in this atomic age, has made millions of humans conscious of a basic insecurity and the need for a tie with a power that no nuclear bomb or any other force can destroy. The only such power, obviously, is the power of God—and the only way to reach God is through prayer.

A minister who believed that the business end of the church is also God's business, prayed that seven thousand dollars would be placed in his hands to make a down payment on a piece of property needed for church expansion. He received no immediate answer following his prayer, so he retired for the night in the faith that he would awaken with the answer. He had carefully gone over the names of all church members and knew none of them could be approached in this emergency. Help would have to come from an outside source, and soon, because the property adjoining the church would be sold to another party.

Upon awakening, the name of a certain well-to-do lady, a prominent member of another church, flashed into the minister's mind. He had briefly met her on a social occasion some months before, but he now found himself strongly tempted to phone her and tell her of his problem. He fought the idea for a time because it seemed so far-fetched. His conscious mind argued that this woman would not be interested in any church but her own, that he was not well enough acquainted to appeal to her for help, and that it would be time wasted, if not embarrassing, to make such a call.

The minister prayed again, waited in the silence, and received the same answer, stronger than before. He had trained himself to follow direction when the "inner voice" spoke to him, so he martialed all the nerve he had and got the lady on the phone.

"How much do you need?" she asked, when he had stated his problem.

"Seven thousand dollars," he replied.

"I'm putting a check for seven thousand in the mail," said the lady. "Make your own terms. I'm glad to be able to help."

Countless businessmen can testify that God has helped them solve their financial problems when they have exhausted their own resources. This minister would never have consciously thought of this woman, but when he freed his mind and left the problem with God to provide the supply, he was given the urge to contact her.

L.S., a builder, discovered that his two partners were dishonest and had robbed him of several hundred thousand dollars. He could have sued them, creating quite a community scandal in the process, and possibly sending the two men to jail. Instead, he took the problem to God in prayer. The answer he got was to rid himself of his two associates and to concentrate his full time and attention on building the business without them. But this was not the answer L.S. had expected. He knew he would have to go to court to recover the large amount of money he had lost; his two partners couldn't and wouldn't pay him back unless they were forced to.

"In a year or two, you will regain this money through your own efforts," an inner voice assured him. "Your partners will be punished enough without your taking action against them. Be thankful you know them for what they are and that you can be free of them from now on."

He decided to follow God's guidance. He said nothing of his intentions, leaving the former partners in a state of anxiety and suspense. They thought, of course, he would have them prosecuted. As time went on, their own feelings of guilt caused one to have a heart attack, the other a nervous breakdown. L.S., relieved of any feelings of bitterness and resentment, because he had released this natural human tendency from his consciousness, devoted all his energies to expanding his business. Today he has achieved greater success than ever before and thanks God every day for giving him the emotional control to avoid legal entanglements and the unpleasantness of months of court action.

A partnership with God in business is the same as taking out insurance against every possible disaster. You know that God is never going to double-cross you, you will never get the wrong counsel. Help is always at hand when you need it. What human partner, however reliable, can afford you such dependable support and guidance?

It has been said that God always answers prayers in one of three ways: yes—no—or wait awhile.

This is well to remember each time you pray. In business, there are times when you are under severe economic pressure, when it seems that you must have an instant answer and no answer is forthcoming. It is then that a feeling wells up in consciousness which translates itself into the words: wait awhile!

Don't try to force an answer under these circumstances. It simply means that, however urgent you think things are, God knows that some new developments are on the way and that they will alter the whole picture and help provide the right solution to the problem. For you to decide on any course of immediate action would be ruinous. You need time to get the true perspective, so God simply gives you no answer. He says, instead, in feelings you cannot mistake, "Wait awhile."

A New England floor-covering industry was going out of business because its markets were disappearing. The owner of the company needed to overhall his entire plant and redesign the machines to go into production on new products. He lacked the money to do it, and it appeared as though he would have to shut down and discharge several hundred employees.

He took the problem to God in prayer. God told him to call a mass meeting of his workers and to discuss his situation with them, and to ask them to pray with him about it.

Out of this meeting came an offer on the part of the employees to help finance the changeover into a new line of products, to work for half salary until the change was made, then to get the rest of their salary when the company got back on a profit-making basis. God moved in the minds and hearts of all concerned and brought about a solution which saved the company, the jobs of the employees, and brought about a fellowship between labor and management which had never existed before.

The right mental attitude of executives and workers is important to every business.

Introduction of the prayer formula into the business life of many firms and industries has revolutionized them in cooperation and understanding.

You cannot stay at odds with people when you are praying with them. You are compelled to adjust your difficulties and to work on your own faults. You know, too, that God isn't going to help you get what you want if you are selfishly opposing someone else's getting what he wants and needs.

Make a business of taking God into partnership with you in all your enterprises, little or big. He is as near to you as a telephone or a push button. You can reach Him—with a prayer!

X

Prayers for the Alcoholic

Because prayer is such a power in the life of an alcoholic, it deserves a special chapter devoted to its function in this field of human need alone.

It is well for you to know, if you are not already aware of it, that every man or woman who has eventually become an alcoholic has been excessively sensitive to some unhappy or trying experience in life. This excessive sensitivity, in turn, has led to an excessive urge for drink.

Such sensitivity, or too intense an emotional reaction to something that has happened, may have started in childhood. It may have grown out of feelings of inferiority, resentment, rebellion against people and circumstances, fears and worries, guilt complexes, economic strains—any one or more of a number of disturbing human experiences.

There is a way for you to judge whether or not you have become or are becoming an excessively sensitive person. If you have let some individual or situation upset you so much emotionally that you can't forget it, that you keep brooding about it or worrying about it, that you begin developing a desire to get away from it all to bolster your courage or defiance, this proves that you have become excessively sensitive. And this is the time to look out, because you have reached the stage of emotional disturbance wherein you are now a potential candidate, if you drink, for becoming an alcoholic!

Once liquor has become your prop against your troubles, real or imaginary, you are like a man in deep water without a life preserver. You may be able to float for a time but you will flounder again and again, and almost drown, taking everything you hold dear down with you. You will cling to loved ones and friends as long as you can. But finally most, if not all of them, will break loose from you for their own self-protection, and you will be left to struggle on alone. It is a sad but true fact that after you are so far gone, those who love you most can help you least. You may turn against their love and their attempts to aid as a defensive gesture or in a resentful leave-me-alone mood, or your pride may be so hurt that you want to avoid them and seek solace in flight, hoping somehow that you can get hold of yourself and regain your self-respect and their respect for you.

There is no experience in human life so tragic and so sordid as the alcoholic or drug habit. All manner of attempted cures have been developed by medical science, and some of the new medicines are making a valued contribution to the control of emotions and mental and psychological disturbances; but every alcoholic knows he can keep free from domination by liquor only as long as he can keep from the next drink.

The greatest discovery yet made in the psychology of alcoholism is the fact that an individual, once he becomes an alcoholic, no longer has the power, in and of himself, to break the habit. To regain control of himself—mentally, emotionally, and physically—he must appeal to a higher power within him: the power of God.

As a result of this discovery by two

men, themselves alcoholics, the wonderful organization known as Alcoholics Anonymous was born. It was set up on the premise that it requires an alcoholic to understand an alcoholic, and that any man or woman who considers their case hopeless can best be helped by people like them, who have fought themselves back to a state of sobriety through reliance upon a power greater than themselves—and who can show them how to do likewise.

In my opinion, there is no human service organization in the world today which approaches Alcoholics Anonymous. Thousand of fine lives, seemingly lost, have been reclaimed and rehabilitated through the selfless, inspired program of these A.A. groups, functioning quietly and effectively in countless communities. They have alleviated untold misery and grief and have aided in restoring many broken homes and families.

There was a minister in the city of Little Rock who one Sunday preached a sermon which made the members of his congregation squirm with uneasiness and chagrin.

He said, "Suppose there should come to your door a man or a woman of seemingly disreputable character, bleary-eyed, dirty, disheveled, breath reeking with alcohol, to ask for aid. Would you take him in, give him a bath, hot coffee, something to eat, then put him to bed and watch over him through the night administering to his every need? In addition to this, would you cancel social and business appointments the next day and stay by the unfortunate's side, giving physical, mental, and spiritual help as required? Not only that, would you call in understanding friends to take turns serving this stranger, staying with him until he was strong enough to go out on his own, well on the way to rehabilitation? Raise your hands, please, any of you who would be such a Good Samaritan?"

Not one hand was raised, of course. And then the pastor said, "But there is an organization in existence whose members, men and womenn, are doing just that for the strangers who come to their doors. This organization is known as Alcoholics Anonymous and, in my judgment, it is the most Christlike human service group in the world today. It puts to shame the puny services to mankind which we are rendering with our donations, rather than with our hands and our spirits. In my considered opinion, not until we really learn to go all out in doing for others, not until we place the high, fine value on each human soul that these people do, can we ever hope to have a better world.

"We can call ourselves Christians, but the word itself will have a hollow, meaningless ring to it. And we who have not been tested by such bitter life experiences had best put aside our feelings of smugness and superiority in the presence of those who have tasted the dregs and have risen to the heights through knowing reliance upon God's power.

"We can learn some of life's greatest lessons in courage, faith, and a demonstration of spiritual principles from those who answer proudly to the roll call of recovered alcoholics."

If you are an alcoholic, or should you have an alcoholic in your family, what I will say from this point on should be particularly helpful.

You, as a member of the family of an alcoholic, can certainly do no less than a stranger would do for your loved one. You should be at least as patient, as considerate, as long-suffering, however difficult the situation. It is true that many alcoholics are psychologically so bound up in emotional disturbances involving wife or husband or children, in-laws, and other relatives, that an understanding stranger, such as a member of an Alcoholics Anonymous group, can do more for them than you can.

But the maintaining of home ties is important. If an alcoholic is cut off completely from his family when he is trying to recover (even though temporarily separated), it may mean years more of misery for all concerned. No human is perfect. But for a more fortuitous act of fate, *we* might, at this moment, be in the place of an alcoholic friend or relative.

There is great healing power in forgiveness—none in condemnation. Never forget that.

If you are an alcoholic, there is no hope for your recovery until you admit to yourself and at least one other person that you are powerless to help yourself. This is a difficult admission to make, and many excessive drinkers refuse to surrender their wills to the higher Will within, for months and years—carrying on the tragic pretense that they are *not* alcoholics, that they can quit any time they want to quit, when everyone who knows them has long since recognized their inability to drink in moderation.

Are you ready to make this admission? If

you are, you have taken the first step toward your recovery. The moment you say to yourself, "God help me, I cannot do it alone," you have joined forces with the greatest power there is. And if you stay with this resolution, in time you will overcome the urge to drink.

I present to you three powerful affirmations, to repeat as needed when you pray. You are to make these thoughts a part of your consciousness, accept them on faith until they become a reality to you. By so doing, you will prepare your mind and heart to receive the answers to prayer which the God-power within will bring to you as soon as you have earned the right to have them.

The first affirmation is designed to relax your mind and body from the tensions you have built up—which tensions you may have been seeking to release through recourse to alcohol. The following affirmations, however, will prove highly beneficial, if feelingly expressed, whether or not you have a drinking problem. Say to yourself, and mean it:

I now let go of all fear and worry thoughts.
I let go of all tense nerves and muscles.
I let go of all feelings of resentment, all memory of anything sad or unhappy.

I take hold of the God-power within me.

I let it fill my mind and my body with its restful, inspiring, protective radiance.

And I know that this God-power will watch over me as I sleep, and that I will awake in the morning refreshed and ready for the new day, each day stronger in body, mind, and spirit.

This second affirmation is to be used when you feel strangely, desperately alone, possibly friendless and deserted, when it may seem that you have little or nothing to which to cling. Actually you are never alone, never deserted, and you must remind yourself of this fact by saying:

I am not alone.

God, the Father, is always with me.

My soul, my identity—that something which says, "I am, I" to me—is an eternal gift from God, the Father.

I can never lose my self because this self is a part of God, and God has a great purpose in life for me which He is revealing, day by day, as I grow in strength of body, mind, and spirit.

I am well and strong. I have the power to

overcome all things within me.

In God's care, no harm can befall me.

I now give myself over to God's protection in sleep, and I will follow His guidance day by day.

The third affirmation is the one to be used nightly when you feel that you are on the right track. It is a declaration of your faith in God and your desire for daily self-development. You may use your own words to express these same thoughts if they come more naturally to you. But you should *feel* each statement, with deep inner conviction, quietly, with no forcing.

Let go all physical and mental tension; in fact, as you relax body and mind, it would be well to say to yourself, "Let go, let God!"

This suggestion will help induce a feeling of greater receptivity as you repeat:

I am well and strong.

I have a perfect nervous system.

A part of God, the Great Intelligence, dwells within me. I can call upon this God-power any time I wish, to help me meet and solve my problems in life.

The past no longer has any hold over me.

I hold no resentment toward any person.

I am going to profit from all of my past experiences and find increasing opportunity, each day, for devoting my talents and services to others.

With this thought, I now relax my body and my mind in the care and guidance of God, the Great Intelligence, working for and through me, knowing that I will sleep soundly and awake in the morning refreshed and ready for the new day.

A conscientious practice of this mental technique, during moments of prayer and meditation, will deepen your faith, increase your knowledge of self, and stabilize your nerves. Accept this on faith—then prove it to yourself.

Once you are attuned to the God-power within you, you are on the certain road to complete recovery. Do not try to travel this road all at once. Take it a day at a time, a prayer at a time, and you will climb it slowly, surely, with no turning back. Even so, the journey will not be easy, but these affirmations and your prayers are the dependable guideposts which can keep you in touch with your unfailing source of strength—the God-power within.

Hundreds of excessive drinkers have reported their success to me. One of the many had this to say:

"I was not only an alcoholic, I was a drug addict. I started on phenobarbital, and graduated to sodium amytal, then went on the nembutals and finally to seconal. I estimate that I have taken from twenty-five to thirty thousand one-and-one-half grain capsules in the past eight years! I was in and out of hospitals and in constant domestic trouble, as you can surmise. At last I decided to have myself committed to a hospital in St. Louis. There I met a doctor who was an alcoholic. He heard my story and then told me, 'You haven't got a chance in the world. Every hospital will turn you out when they learn your history. Your only hope is God.'

"I couldn't claim any close acquaintanceship with God, in fact I hadn't believed in God, but when this doctor explained the organization of Alcoholics Anonymous to me and told what God was doing for its members, he aroused my interest. I discovered that I had needed someone to take a real interest in me and to show faith in me. It gave me new hope.

"I stayed with that doctor day and night.

He wouldn't take any money, but he let me visit him in his home and in the office. He took me out to dinner and on his calls. I asked myself, 'Why would anyone put himself out like this to save a no-account like me? Maybe I'm worth more than I think I am. I *must* be worth salvaging or he wouldn't spend all this time on me.'

"I began going to meetings of the Alcoholics Anonymous group, deciding if he was doing all this for me, I should start doing something for myself. In February of 1953, I took my last drink, and I had already knocked out the drugs. It's impossible to describe the horrors I went through, not only while I was drinking and taking drugs, but when I was fighting to get free of it.

"I'd be lying if I said it was easy. It's not easy yet to keep free; it's a battle every day. But I've got the faith and the will to fight back now. Whenever I feel myself weakening, I get busy and set up my pipeline to God, through prayer, and He gives me the power to resist.

"Why am I telling you this? Because I want you to pass along the good word. Tell everybody who thinks they can't lick a liquor or drug habit that it can be done.

"You have to work at it—but you can be very sure that if I came out on top you can, because I was as low as I could get!"

Yes, he was low as all alcoholics are—until they turn to God in prayer, ask His help, and He lifts them up.

Prepare your mind now so that you develop the kind of thoughts and feelings which will enable God to manifest Himself through you. The longer you put it off, the more difficult it will be. Today is the only time there is. Do what you know you should today, and tomorrow will take care of itself. Pray to God that it will, with His help.

XI

Prayers for the Family

Sincere reverence for God, expressed through prayer in a family group, is always inspiring to see. It is an unforgettable experience to have been or to be a member of such a family group. It matters not what the religious faith, it is the spirit with which all enter into communion with God, the Father, on these family occasions, which is so deeply impressive.

My father was not a religious man in any narrow, denominational sense. He definitely believed in what might be termed "One Flock, One Shepherd," a God so cosmic in scope that He embraced all life and creatures, not only on this little earth, but throughout His unthinkably vast kingdom of universes. And yet my father felt that it was possible for us, in some miraculous but simple way, to make personal contact with God, the Great Intelligence, through prayer. But he would engage in family prayers only on special occasions, believing that the primary function of prayer was intended as a direct line of communication between an individual and his Maker.

The times that my father did pray, therefore, stand out in my memory. They were the prayers of a man who had pondered much on the mysteries of the universe and the nature of God, and they were spoken in words filled with meaning. Father could not stand what he termed "the flowery attempts of some ministers to flatter the Creator." He told me once that he did not like to hear the word *God* used often, for this reason, because "the greatest mistake we make is our minds' finite conception of such an infinite power and intelligence, and the word *God*, as a consequence, is used to profane rather than to proclaim our Creator."

Certainly, it serves no good purpose to rattle off prayers as a duty when the family gathers about the dinner table, giving no respectful thought to what is being said.

On Broadway there was once a play titled

You Can't Take It With You, in which a grandfather was called upon to say grace every time the lively family group was assembled for a meal. His opening salutation was, "Well, God, here we are again!" After a short acknowledgement, the family got the "go" sign and it was everyone for himself.

You have been present at family dinners when the father or mother or a grandparent or some other member would recite a prayer with such speed or in such a low voice that you couldn't make out what was said. Heads were bowed and raised so fast that no reverence could be implied, let alone expressed.

It would be better, unless such sincere attention is given to the blessing, not to speak it at all. A simple bowing of the heads, if any outward recognition is bestowed upon the Giver of all gifts, would enable all present to inwardly express thanks in a more effective way than a mere parroting of words.

You may have been present at a family gathering when time was taken for a moment of silence, or a short, thoughtful prayer was uttered, which came from the heart and reached all hearts, and lifted the spirits of all to the level of God consciousness within.

Robert Louis Stevenson loved his home and loved his family. He was a believer in prayer and the participation of the family in prayer, but he also believed that a prayer should say something and express the true feeling of all present.

When he had concluded his South Sea wanderings and established his home on one of the Samoa Islands, it was his custom, each Sunday evening, to gather his household together for prayers. "Family Prayer" is one of the many that he wrote for these simple services.

Lord, behold our family here assembled. We thank Thee for this place in which we dwell; for the love that unites us; for the peace accorded us this day; for the hope with which we expect the morrow; for the health, the work, the food, and the bright skies, that make our lives delightful; for our friends in all parts of the earth, and our friendly helpers in this foreign isle.

Give us grace and strength to forbear and to persevere . . . . give us courage and gaiety and the quiet mind. Spare to us our friends, soften to us our enemies. Bless us, if it may be, in all our innocent endeavours. If it may not, give us strength to encounter that which is to come, that we be brave in peril, constant in tribulation, temperate in wrath, and in all changes of fortune and, down to the gates of death, loyal and loving to one another.

How can you be in the presence of one uttering such a prayer and not be touched by it, not have your own heart and life warm to it, and not reach out with a yearning toward God, the Father, to be worthy of receiving an answer to this petition?

No wonder all who gathered at Robert Louis Stevenson's festive board, and were included as members of his household, felt especially privileged and blessed during these inspired moments of communion with the God Presence.

The life of a family is a constant variety show of comedy and tragedy, joy and sorrow, good happenings and bad. All of this is reflected in the nature of the prayers offered up individually and collectively. A family group trained to look to God for guidance by the example of a reverent father and mother can stand together through crises much easier than one in which there is little or no faith in the protective influence of a higher power.

Many families have a divided allegiance to

God. The mother may be a believer in prayer, the father not; but it is more often the woman who steers the family ship of state in spiritual matters, which is the reason that so many men and women speak of having learned to pray "at their mother's knee."

Today we are living in a era of noise and confusion. Almost every home has both a radio and a television set operating at all hours. Recording machines are playing the latest pop tunes. The younger set are rushing around with hardly time to put their feet under the family dinner table at the same moment. Mothers and fathers are equally busy with clubs, churches, social activities, various types of entertainment, sporting events, and recreation, as well as business. With these demands upon young and old, each has little time for the other, let alone time for God. In many homes, if a father or mother attempted to start a new custom by saying grace before eating, they would be dubbed "old hat" and chided for holding up the parade.

Let an accident take place, however, and in the presence of a possible death in the family, everyone gives sober thought to God. The minister calls and prays for the injured loved one; friends call and pray or promise to pray; and members of the family resort to prayer. But the moment the accident victim is on the road to recovery, and the apparent need for the "insurance policy" is over, praying is put back on the shelf until another emergency. It is an umbrella for the rainy day—and who needs God while the sun is shining?

Part of the reason for the lack of more prayers in the home is the fact that prayers are not considered to be of practical, everyday value by many people. They have the idea that you go to God in trouble, and why bother Him when everything is all right? But if they could realize that they create their own troubles by wrong thinking, and that looking to their God-power within for guidance each day would enable them to eliminate the causes of most troubles before they materialize, every sensible person would set aside time for prayer.

If young people were taught that when they pray for something they want they are actually creating a picture in their mind's eye, and that this picture is developed by the God-given creative power through their exercise of faith into a reality—they would give enthusiastic attention to prayer.

We creatures are innately selfish. We have a "what's in it for me?" philosophy. We run after the biggest jackpot contests and the biggest giveaway programs. Would we turn more quickly to God if we had Him pictured to us as the greatest Giver of all? Every good thing you have ever had, starting with the gift of life itself, has come essentially from God. What you will be tomorrow and what you will have tomorrow is up to you—and God.

It is seldom that all members of a family want the same thing at the same time because of their varying interests and needs. Occasionally everyone in the family agrees that it is time for some common piece of property such as a new car. If Dad can't afford to buy it and there are other working members of the family, they may chip in to help get it. Perhaps all their resources combined still can't purchase the desired automobile. A family circle believing in prayer would then ask God to help provide the opportunity to secure the means to get the car. Each member would picture this car as he prayed, and see himself doing everything possible to earn the money to make the car a reality.

There is power in such family prayer

because all minds and hearts are united on one objective and have harnessed the God-power in each to the God-power in the other. They have put deep feeling behind it because a car is something they all very much want. This feeling intensifies their faith and sets up magnetic action in consciousness which begins attracting to them the resources they need to produce the car for them.

You and your family could attain many more worthwhile things in life if you made known your aspirations and needs to each other and combined the power of your prayers.

And each would have to pray just as unselfishly for the other as for himself. If jealousy or covetousness exists in the mind of some family members, it will set up an inharmonious condition in consciousness and counteract the effective operation of the God-given creative power which helps materialize what is desired.

You cannot know what is in the mind of another. He may tell you that he is praying for one thing when he is secretly desirous of something else. Since like always attracts like in the realm of mind, as has been emphasized, you eventually get what you desire or pray for—in some form, either individually or collectively. Therefore, be sure you are really praying for what you want, that you are not deceiving yourself.

A young woman told me that she felt she was not appreciated at home, and she prayed that a way would open up so she could leave home. She loved her mother and hated her father. She told herself that she wanted to leave home so she could get work and earn money and help her mother have a better life. But her real reason was a desire to be out on her own and stay out late nights and have a good time and escape the discipline imposed by the father. Because she was not honest with herself, she got the wrong answer to her prayer. A man propositioned her to run away with him and get married. She looked upon this as the opportunity she was awaiting. The man seduced her and abandoned her, without marriage. When she returned home, her mother told her that she knew she had been restless and dissatisfied for some time, and that she had been secretly praying that her daughter would find some way she could leave home and get what she wanted. The mother's prayer was as unintelligent as the daughter's had been. The way to leave home was provided in answer to prayer, but it was not the right way.

You must know what is really in the mind and heart of another person before you ask God to grant them what they want. The God-given creative power may grant it when it is not for the good of the individual because the individual's thinking and desires are wrong. It is dangerous to pray for what you inwardly know you don't want, because if you believe you will get it, you will! And if well-meaning members of the family help you pray for the same thing, lacking comprehension of what its realization might do to you, they are only speeding the day when it will happen.

I had an aunt who prayed that the members of her family would stay under one roof after they were grown, and continue to work and support her husband and herself. To her, it represented a happy, prosperous arrangement. She knew that if her sons and daughters married and had homes of their own, it would radically alter her own standard of living.

What she should have done was to have prayed unselfishly that her children would find the right mates and great happiness in their own lives. Instead, she made known her desires to her sons and daughters and talked against any of their friends who began to show a romantic interest. She prayed fervently that God would not let her children be taken from her—that He would preserve the "happy family."

This "happy family" became more and more unhappy; the love of some of the children turned to hate toward the mother as marital opportunities were lost. In time, all left the home, despite the mother's tearful reminder of all she had done for them, the sacrifices she had made to maintain their home all these years, and now, in the twilight of their father's and her lives, they were walking out on her. This was the reward she was getting for her devotion!

This, of course, is the wrong use of prayer as applied to family life. The God-given creative power acts upon the prayers you present. It is up to you to present the right ones. Had this mother prayed for care and protection for herself and husband, irrespective of what the children decided to do, she would have found an answer to her needs, whatever happened.

As it was, most of the children felt so antagonistic, when they married they did not want the mother in their homes. They were not disposed to do things for her, since she had sought to control their lives and to keep them from establishing homes of their own.

You cannot influence God to take sides when you pray that someone who has hurt you be punished, and that someone else who has helped you be rewarded. It is highly possible that you have contributed your share to the hurt and that the individual you wish rewarded has sympathized unduly with you. The God-given creative power lets you draw on its substance as you desire it and ask for it—and, believing, you receive it. But if you get something that you discover through experience has not been good for you, don't blame God for it. You shouldn't have asked for it in the first place.

A family is a complex institution of many desires and needs. If everyone in the family unit prayed earnestly and humbly each day for guidance, expressing the desire to be shown how to help the others so that all could realize more happiness, that would be a happy household indeed.

It has been demonstrated that families who pray together usually manifest greater love for each other and that this love is reflected in a love of God, which, in turn is productive of greater all-around happiness and security.

XII

Prayers for All Peoples

Throughout history, God has never been given a chance to rule in the hearts and minds of all men. This has been the dream of spiritual leaders in all ages. Can such a dream ever come true? Are the forces of good and evil to remain in eternal warfare on this planet? Where a vast number of people of diverse beliefs are concerned, you cannot expect to achieve a harmonious result in a short time. Like drops of rain falling incessantly, the spiritual face of the world will be changed only bit by bit.

To do this will require great faith and patience, because at times it will seem that no progress is being made. You have found, no doubt, that it has required great faith and patience for you to bring about needed changes in your own life.

Plato, one of the world's greatest philosophers, made this wise observation: *As the soul or mind moves, so does everything else in the universe move in relation thereto.* This is just as true today. Plato recognized the power of mind to create the future destiny of mankind, the power of mind to affect the entire universe, as well as the individual.

It is well to remember that "truth is truth to the end of reckoning." The interpretation of truth may be different in different ages, but what really is, is! We may learn more about the truth, how better to adapt ourselves to it, and we may change, but the law doesn't—truth remains truth.

Since we cannot change the laws of the universe, the laws of God, it is about time that we decided to abide by them, to spiritualize our minds through prayer so that we can work with the laws of God instead of against them.

Here is a prayer that might help you establish an understanding relationship with God and His laws:

Our Father,

I thank You for the abiding presence of Your own consciousness within me, for the eternal "I am" which tells me that I am an unfolding, evolving part of all that is or ever can be.

I thank You for the great privilege You have granted me to serve You through serving others.

I thank You, dear Father, for letting me realize that You are manifesting Your unchanging, eternal laws, Your infinite justice and love, through all forms of nature, the wondrous continuing works of Your boundless heavens and Your human family, of which I am a humble member.

I thank You for the opportunity which is forever mine to seek, through free choice, the experiences which lead unfailingly toward greater and greater perfection of my evolving soul.

And as I enlarge my consciousness through experience, I thank You for opening my spiritual eyes so that I can see that all my human ills are caused by wrong thinking, and that the only path to peace and happiness and understanding lies in ridding my mind and heart of such thoughts.

And last, dear Father, when my life is ready to withdraw from this earth, and my body returns to the original particles from which it was made, I thank You for the faith that you will be with my soul as it journeys to the new life awaiting me in the world beyond.

In the exercise of faith, you need to know that faith is not just a word, a symbol, or an attitude—it is a force!

Whenever you call upon your faith you start the mightiest power in the world in action, the power of your own mind. This power draws, in turn, upon the God-power which indwells your consciousness. There is no language by which this power can be described, except to suggest that it is electromagnetic in nature—that it takes your mental picture of what you desire and attracts the conditions, resources, circumstances, even the people you need to meet, to help make what you have pictured become reality.

Nothing moves until faith is first exercised. Faith is the activator. But the functioning of faith can be either constructive or destructive. If, through fear, you have faith that something bad is going to happen, you will cause the power within to attract it. This power makes no distinction between good and bad—it produces for you what you believe in.

Therefore, when we say "all things are possible to those who believe," we mean just that. If you believe in something that isn't good for you and if you persist in this belief, you will eventually get it!

If Dr. Salk had doubted his ability to develop a successful polio vaccine, he could not have done it. He would have abandoned his research. If Edison had doubted his power to invent an electric bulb, he would have quit long before he completed ten thousand unsuccessful experiments in an effort to find the right filament. If Einstein had thought he could not solve the atomic riddle of the universe, he would not have persisted with his profound mathematical equations.

If—but whenever you use that word it is too late, because what happened *did* happen. You cannot go back and re-do what you did. You can only profit by extracting the lessons past experience has taught you—either how to do or how not to do something; this is the value of experience. You have only to place your unfaltering faith behind your prayers for achievement and you will ultimately arrive at your goal in life. It may take years of disappointment and apparent failure, but out of seeming adversity success is always born!

This holds true for the individual as well as the group, if faith is maintained until the objective is reached.

The lives of great men and women testify to their exercise of faith—they believed steadfastly in themselves and in the power within them. They believed when all others may have lost faith in them; they dared ridicule, criticism, even punishment, persecution, and death. Their faith was strong enough to withstand all this, to see them through to final victory.

Perhaps you will never be considered great in the eyes of the world. Few of the truly great men and women set out with the conscious desire to become great. They had a worthwhile objective in life in which they believed, and the attainment of these ambitions brought them distinction.

It is worth reemphasizing these points:

Your faith can take you where you want to go if you are willing to put forth every effort in support of that faith. The Bible emphatically states that "faith without works is dead." All experience bears out the truth of this statement.

If you are not willing to work to help attain what you profess to believe in and what you are praying for, then your faith is only wishful thinking. You can analyze the degree of intensity of your own faith in any project by asking yourself, "How hard am I willing to work to gain success in this undertaking?" You'll get your answer in a hurry. If you do not sense an immediate enthusiastic response, a spontaneous urge, a fervent desire, a compelling drive in the direction of your goal, you're only hoping you will one day arrive—you don't really believe it.

There is a positive quality about genuine faith. It quiets your fears and worries, it stills impatience, it soothes irritations and disappointments, it helps sustain emotional stability in the face of life's ups and downs. To be successful and to remain successful, you must have faith. Occasionally people who have suffered setbacks have lost their faith. In losing it, they have lost their power to recover from a disaster, such as a fire which may have destroyed their business or industry or home.

"I used to be able to picture what I wanted and then go out and get it," many people say to me. "But after what's happened to me, I can't do it any more."

"Why not?" I ask them. "You've got the

same power within you which brought your success in the first place."

"Yes," they lament, "but I don't have the same faith."

That's it: the power remains, but the faith is gone; and without faith, the power lies useless. It cannot function except in the negative, without faith. Lack of faith really means that you *believe* you are helpless to do anything about an unhappy situation you may be in. Such a belief will only perpetuate your helplessness and further aggravate your condition.

All human progress starts with faith. All faith is fulfilled by work. You've heard the story of the woman who had read in the Bible that faith could move mountains. She was on a western trip and was spending the night in a motel which looked out upon a mountain range. When she retired that night, as a test of faith, she prayed that when she awakened in the morning, she would find that the mountain had been removed. Upon arising, she rushed to the window and looked out. The mountain range was still there. "Oh, well," she said, "just as I thought!"

The seemingly mountainous obstacles in your path can be removed by faith—if you will unite your efforts with that faith. It may take a fleet of bulldozers in the form of long and sustained hard work to cut through the barriers between you and the success which awaits you, but it can be done. You have the power to do it if you operate on the principle and with the positive conviction that "all things are possible to him who believes."

Having exercised your faith in support of your prayer for something you need or wish, then waiting for it to come to pass—after you have done all you possibly could to help make it happen—is one of the toughest assignments in life. This is doubly true when you are under economic pressure, when you have to get results by a certain time in order to obtain the money to pay your bills.

The tendency is to get in there and push, to write a letter or make a phone call, or drop in on the party (accidentally, on purpose) who has to act on your proposition; anything to move the deal along, to speed it up. And yet, nine times out of ten, your attempt to get quicker action may produce the opposite effect and slow the deal up and even kill it. You must manage, somehow, to find the patience and the faith in the God-power within to give it the time to do its work.

A farmer knows better than to dig his plantings up to see if they have started to grow. He doesn't overfertilize or overcultivate his crops. He knows that nature must be allowed a reasonable length of time, given a fair amount of rain and sunshine, to sprout the seeds and develop what he has planted. But people are unpredictable. They change their minds, go cold on a proposition, or get interested in something else entirely. They have accidents or get sick, which prevents them from doing what you are counting on. This all spells possible delay in the completion of a project, so the returns you have hoped to realize are delayed.

Never put all your eggs in one basket. It pays to be resourceful—not to have to count on just one source of help materializing.

Rather than remain idle while waiting for the consummation of negotiations, it is well, after you have prayed for results, to put your mind and your efforts on something else. When days go by and you hear nothing either good or bad about your prospects, it is easy to begin imagining the worst. You are sure things aren't going to work out, that all your efforts have been in vain, that you've wasted valuable time and money. Every time the telephone rings or the mailman comes, you know it's bringing the dreaded word that everything is off.

The unhappy fact is, if you let yourself get into a pessimistic, negative mood, your attitude may influence others to go negative, too, especially if they aren't too optimistic in the first place. Then, if they fail to fulfill their end of the bargain, you say to them, "Well, I lost confidence in the deal anyway," and they reply, "That's just the way I began to feel about it."

If you believe in something you have done with or for somebody else—and it is now up to them to carry on—maintain a positive attitude. Give them every encouragement, every benefit of every doubt. Picture this job being followed through to a successful conclusion.

"I wish I hadn't let So-and-So in on this deal," people have said to me. "I don't have much faith that they can finish it. I don't think they know what they're doing. They're not moving fast enough to suit me. They should have gotten results long ago. I haven't heard from them in days. You can't tell me they're getting anywhere."

Perhaps, sometimes such feelings are justified. But it rarely helps for you to find fault with your associates or prospects, though it is hard to sit on the sidelines when you have done your part, and leave it to the other fellow to do his.

A salesman makes his proposition and the prospect says he will think it over and let him know, and the salesman doesn't hear from the man. A real estate operator shows a potential buyer a piece of property, and the prospective client says he will make up his mind in a few days, but the days go by and he receives no word.

When and how should the salesman and the real estate operator make the next approach? Should they permit overanxiety, lack of patience, to cause them to try to exert pressure, to get on the trail of their prospects and hound them until they have said yes or no? In cases like these, if you can control your feelings, if you can come to know yourself well enough so you can tell, through *feeling,* that impatience is not dictating your attitude—then you will be able to decide the right time to go into action. Pray that the God-power within will give you the proper urge or hunch, reveal to you through your intuition what to do and when to do it.

There is a sense of timing in those who have

conquered impatience and possess sufficient faith which always gives them the go-ahead at the right moment. Until this inner signal comes they know it is foolhardy to proceed.

Go fishing, play golf or tennis—do anything, but don't go near the people you are counting on to do something for you. They are not ready to respond yet; they haven't finished their end of the job. You rush them at your own expense—and possibly theirs. Be patient, knowing that no genuine effort is ever lost in the long run; that you will get your compensation for work well done, even though at times the other fellow fails you.

This same faith and patience must be employed when you join with others to pray for world betterment. As your contribution to the advanced thought of the world you should start now praying for the brotherhood of all which must come if we are to survive. Start putting into the stream of consciousness your own love and good will toward others. Think of the evil thoughts of hate and lust and murder and prejudice and other destructive feelings which are flooding the minds of millions! You can combat them only by adding to the sum total of good thoughts. A pinch of salt dropped into a glass of water can almost instantly be tasted. Your own thinking will not be lost in the great sea of consciousness.

Pray earnestly and pray often for the good of all, because, by so doing, you are improving your own condition in life. You can be certain that without your knowledge many people in many lands are praying for you. They desire peace and understanding as much as you do, and they are as concerned as you are about the future.

If it were possible for all the peoples of the world to stop and devote five tremendous minutes to the heartfelt expression of goodwill toward one another—uttering a prayer that humankind might live in peace and understanding from that second on—the impact of this harmonized thought of billions of souls would be incalculable. There have been different world prayer movements with some such idea in mind, but they have not reached out to all religions and all peoples. Unfortunately, too much segregation still exists between various races and faiths for all to agree and cooperate wholeheartedly on such a project.

It would require colossal organization and equally colossal publicity to arouse the masses of all countries to give expression to a world prayer for peace and understanding and goodwill. There is not yet sufficient realization of the great power of prayer to cause people to join their minds and hearts in a tidal wave of tolerant, loving feelings toward each other and toward their concepts of God. If there were, the problems of humanity could be solved in an incredibly short span of time.

The refusal to surrender outmoded ideas and traditions which have long ago lost their usefulness, and which, in many instances, have held back advancement, has kept the human race from becoming one happy family on this planet. You cannot pray for world peace and have hatred in your mind and heart for people of another race, color, or religion.

The prayer of a Sioux Indian chief was chosen for use in the "World Day of Prayer" which was observed by churches in a hundred and thirty-four foreign countries as well as in twenty thousand American communities, and which has been an annual event from the time of its origination in 1887 to the time of this writing. This prayer, repeated by millions, was written by the late Yellow Lark. It placed the emphasis where it belongs—on the individual!—and calls for a change in your own mind and heart before a change can be expected in the mind and heart of another toward you.

Oh, Great Spirit, whose voice I hear in the winds, and whose breath gives life to all the world, hear me.

I come before You, one of Your many children. I am small and weak. I need Your strength and wisdom.

Let me walk in beauty and make my eyes ever behold the red and purple sunset. Make my hands respect the things You have made, my ears sharp to hear Your voice.

Make me wise, so that I may know the things You have taught my people, the lesson You have hidden in every leaf and rock.

I seek strength, not to be superior to my brothers, but to be able to fight my greatest enemy, myself.

Make me ever ready to come to You with clean hands and straight eyes, so when life fades as a fading sunset, my spirit may come to You without shame.

This is one of the finest prayers ever uttered, and if we could repeat it again and again—and mean it—this prayer would keep us in attunement with God consciousness within, and cleanse our body, mind, and spirit.

World movements to invite all people to join in prayer, if motivated by the spirit of Yellow Lark's sublime petition to the Great Spirit, can accomplish much good.

But peace will come only through a change in the minds and hearts of all people. Can we love our neighbor as ourselves? Prayer can help. As the enlightened Sioux emphasized, prayer can help you to seek strength, not to be superior to your brothers, but to be able to fight your greatest enemy, yourself.

XIII

Peace of Mind Through Prayer

What one thing has humankind done which has lifted us above all other life on this planet and set us apart from the rest of creation? From earliest times we have recognized a power higher than ourselves and have reached out in worship and supplication to this power, seeking strength and guidance in moments of danger, strife, confusion, indecision, or fear. When we, however ignorant or enlightened have humbly and earnestly looked to God for help, we have always found the power to face all manner of trials and adversities.

God has spoken to us through our minds, our intuition, our higher sensory faculties, giving us the urge and the courage to meet whatever difficulties confront us, rewarding us according to our faith and willingness to follow the direction of the voice within. We would never have emerged from the primitive state had it not been for prayer.

The God-ward urge dwells in each human heart. It accounts for the restless, unsatisfied, unhappy, insecure feelings many humans have. They know, consciously or unconsciously, that they have lost contact with the God-power within, and that without this contact they have little or no direction in life. They are too often the victims of uncontrolled emotions, destructive feelings of hate, prejudice, resentment, greed, or fear.

There is only one way to escape domination by these feelings. If you are disturbed in mind and heart, you cannot change your condition until you have changed your mind. Remember that the God-power within will not compel you to change. As a creature of free will and free choice, you can choose to use the God-given creative power wrongly if you so desire.

Wrong thoughts will automatically and infallibly produce wrong results, just as right thoughts will as surely produce right results. If at times you have not received the answers for which you have prayed, you can be sure that, somewhere along the line, you have failed to live in harmony with God's laws. It is worth reminding you again that in order to get the right answer to prayer you must make a clear channel of your mind so you are prepared and ready to receive what you have asked for. This may take time, but a very deserving prayer is answered in time, perhaps not in the way you thought it should be answered, but in the right way—if you have sought the answer sincerely and honestly.

Never forget that you cannot deceive God. Your inner self knows whether or not you really mean what you say, whether or not you really want what you profess to want. Keep this fact in the foreground of your mind at all times: a part of God, the Great Intelligence, dwells in your innermost consciousness. You are a part of God, evolving your soul by physical, emotional, mental, and spiritual reactions to what happens to you in this life.

You are living in a universe ruled by cause and effect. You set up the causes by your own thinking, good or bad, and you get the effects in time, of these thoughts. It must then be clear that God does not punish you; you punish yourself.

You now have a technique through a study

of the contents of this book, to get the right answers to prayer—the answers you deserve and desire. Once having learned the right way to pray you will find yourself in tune with the greatest power in the universe—the God-power within you. This power is able to attract to you whatever you need. All you have to do is to picture this need in your mind and support your idea with faith and prayer. But it is necessary, after you have done this, for you to put forth every effort on your own behalf.

A highly successful businessman, whose life is governed by prayer, stresses the importance of backing up faith with works. "The only time our prayers are answered," he declares, "is when we say 'Amen' and then get up and do something about it!"

What are you doing about it? Sitting around, having prayed, waiting for God to do it all? He won't. He will supply you with the ammunition, but you'll have to fire it. You need the assurance in your own mind and heart that God is with you and is helping, but you must work along with Him. You will have attained peace of mind when you come to know this.

When you pray that you may think right

and do right each day, you are actually performing a surgical operation by causing the God-power within to remove wrong mental attitudes while enabling you to assume the right ones. You are creating conditions which protect you against wrong happenings and mishaps, which see to it that you are at the right place at the right time, taking full advantage of the right opportunities, making the right decisions, saying and doing the right things.

But are you grateful for this? Do you fill your heart with gratitude and express it so that your love and appreciation can reach God?

So many of us seek material answer to prayer, forgetting too often to give thought to the sheer joy of living and to all the blessings that are ours.

Once, when I was leaving New York City, I hailed a cab and told the driver to take me to the airport. I was feeling just a bit sorry for myself because certain things had not worked out as I had hoped. Why had certain important people whom I had counted on seeing either been sick or out of town? Why had it taken some publishers and producers so long to give me an answer on my manuscripts?

Why had others made promises which they obviously were not going to keep? What was wrong with the world, anyway? These were my thoughts as I settled back in the cab.

"Airport, did you say?" asked the taxi driver. The sound of his voice took my attention instantly from myself. It seemed to come from his stomach. He swallowed before he spoke. Words came jerkily, and with effort. The voice was hoarse and weak.

Intuitively, I knew what had happened. This man had no voice box. It had been removed because of cancer.

"That's right, mister," he confirmed. "Had an operation three years ago. Took me eight months to learn to talk again. I have to swallow air first—like this—then form the words as the air passes out. Quite a trick!" He smiled. "Got an amplifier here on the seat beside me. I can hook it up to get volume, when I need it. Kind of a nuisance, but it works. Good for my temper . . . can't bawl people out like I used to. Have to save my breath." He chuckled at his own joke as he swung the cab into the freeway and set off on a beeline for the air terminal.

"How long have you been driving a cab?" I asked.

He swallowed several times, then, half-turning toward me, he siphoned out the words.

"All my life. Don't know anything else. Too late to change now. Twenty-two years right here in little old New York. I've *had* it mister . . . but I love it. Sure, it's nerve-racking, but I love it."

"Any family?" I asked.

He swallowed again before answering. "Wife. Good woman. Flat on her back half the time with heart trouble. Got a daughter, too."

"Married?"

"Naw, she's still home. Thirty-three years old—still six in her mind. She'll never marry. Fell on her head when a kid. Injured her brain—plays with dolls. Never be any better."

"Pretty tough," I couldn't help saying.

"It could have been worse," he rasped, between breaths. "I could have died. I'm thankful God let me live so I can keep on drivin' this cab. Every night, when I pray, I say, 'God, I ain't askin' no favors . . . I ain't tryin' to understand why these things had to happen . . . I'm just askin' please give me the strength to stay on the job.' So far—knock on wood—my prayers have been answered. I'm not kickin'. I got a wonderful wife, and my daughter—each night when I come home she's watchin' out the window for me. She's sweet. Well, what you gonna do? It don't help to gripe about it. I'm just thankful, like I said, to be alive."

Thankful to be alive—with burdens like those! I said a prayer of my own in his cab. "Thank You, God, for putting me in this taxi, for giving me this new perspective."

Back on the West Coast, where I was then living, I went to my attorney for some advice on a contract. I had great admiration for this man; he was in his seventies, alert in mind and body, one of the best-known and most respected men in his profession.

I told him of my experience with the taxi driver. He listened thoughtfully, and then said, "Thank you, Sherman. That's very helpful to me at this time—you don't know how helpful. My wife is an invalid because of a stroke; our only son is a victim of Parkinson's disease and has been bedridden for years. We have been taking care of his two children. Just last week our son's wife, who has become an alcoholic due to the strain of caring for him, fell and broke her leg so badly she will have to be in a cast for months. I guess nothing's so bad that it couldn't have been worse."

I looked at him in amazement, and thought to myself, how little we know the loads others are carrying. What a mistake it is to let our own loads get us down.

"How do you stand up under this and do your work as usual?" I had to ask.

My friend smiled and gave me this simple answer, "What else can you do? The only sensible thing is to accept it and go on."

Accept it and go on! No inner resentment, no loss of faith, no conflict, no attempt at escapism. Just face reality; do the best each day that can be done under the circumstances, thankful merely to be alive.

When the problems of life seem to pile up, when I am tempted to lose patience and to rebel, I think of the taxi driver and of my attorney friend and the host of other people like them, and I say to myself, with renewed resolution, "Accept it and go on!" You have no idea, until you try it, how much lighter all your burdens instantly become!

D.B., a famous writer of inspirational poetry, wrote to me one time, "I sometimes think that our greatest prayers are those inarticulate ones, when the gratefulness of the heart is almost painful in its upwelling, the mute cry of thanks, and thanks, both for beauty and for the gift of seeing and living it."

You should carry thanksgiving in your mind and heart, from day to day. Offering prayers of gratitude will prove a physical, mental, and spiritual tonic for you. It will remind you, in dark moments, that such moments will pass away, and good things will come again.

Take a moment with me, now, as we near the end of our journey together, to let the feeling of gratitude and thanksgiving fill your entire being as you read and repeat this prayer of gratitude:

Our Father,
My heart is filled to overflowing with a feeling of
gratitude and thanksgiving.
Gratitude for the gift of life to me,
Thanksgiving for the joy of living;
For the good things of earth,
The love and trust of friends and dear ones,
The sweetness and promise of little

children,
The daily opportunity to grow through experience and
To help my fellow humans help themselves,
To rise above failure and disappointment,
To draw from You the strength, the wisdom, and the courage
To meet whatever I may be called upon to face,
In the knowledge and the faith
That You, dear Father, are always with me.
For all this, I am deeply grateful,
Mindful of my dependence upon Your God-given power,
Each minute of each day;
Mindful of my need to keep my thoughts attuned
In harmony with Your indwelling spirit
So that my unfolding life will find
Ever more joyous, healthful, and helpful expression,
As I strive always to live up to the best in me,
To be worthy of your priceless gift—
The possession of my own soul,

My identity as a part of Your everlasting
God consciousness.
For these things and much, very much,
that I can never express in words,
I give You thanks!
Amen

About the Author

Harold Sherman is the founder of ESP Research Associates Foundation in Little Rock, Arkansas, an organization devoted to the exploration of the origin and nature of extrasensory perception.

Sherman has published over sixty books and has lectured in the U.S. and abroad. Besides his many popular books on metaphysical subjects, Sherman has written sports and adventure novels, a screenplay ("The Adventures of Mark Twain," 1942), and two plays that appeared on Broadway ("Her Supporting Cast" and "The Little Black Book"). He was the host of a popular radio program, "Your Key to Happiness," broadcast from New York City and Chicago.

Born in Traverse City, Michigan, in 1898, Sherman attended the University of Michigan and served in World War I. He spent some time in Detroit helping Henry Ford build "Tin Lizzies," then launched his writing career as a reporter at the Marion Chronicle in Marion, Indiana.

Sherman's career has lately been devoted to psychic research. He gained worldwide attention in 1937-38, when he conducted mind-to-mind communication experiments with arctic explorer Sir Hubert Wilkins, who was over 2,000 miles away. Sherman has researched spiritual healing, visualization, and related areas.

Ernest Holmes, author of "Science of Mind," said: "I can wholeheartedly recommend Mr. Sherman's books to all who are in search of self-development."

Sherman and his wife, Martha, live in Mountain View, Arkansas.

Printed U.S.A. 176-F-8752-5M-6-86